CONSTITUTIONAL
AMENDMENTS
BEYOND THE BILL OF RIGHTS

Amendment XIX Granting Women the Right to Vote

Other Books of Related Interest

Opposing Viewpoints Series

Civil Liberties

Feminism

Race Relations

Work

Working Women

Current Controversies Series

Civil Liberties

Extremist Groups

Feminism

Human Rights

CONSTITUTIONAL
AMENDMENTS
BEYOND THE BILL OF RIGHTS

Amendment XIX Granting Women the Right to Vote

Carrie Fredericks, Book Editor

GREENHAVEN PRESS
A part of Gale, Cengage Learning

GALE
CENGAGE Learning™

Detroit • New York • San Francisco • New Haven, Conn • Waterville, Maine • London

Christine Nasso, *Publisher*
Elizabeth Des Chenes, *Managing Editor*

© 2009 Greenhaven Press, a part of Gale, Cengage Learning.

Gale and Greenhaven Press are registered trademarks used herein under license.

For more information, contact:
Greenhaven Press
27500 Drake Rd.
Farmington Hills, MI 48331-3535
Or you can visit our Internet site at gale.cengage.com

For product information and technology assistance, contact us at

Gale Customer Support, 1-800-877-4253
For permission to use material from this text or product, submit all requests online at
www.cengage.com/permissions

Further permissions questions can be emailed to permissionrequest@cengage.com

Articles in Greenhaven Press anthologies are often edited for length to meet page require-ments. In addition, original titles of these works are changed to clearly present the main thesis and to explicitly indicate the author's opinion. Every effort is made to ensure that Greenhaven Press accurately reflects the original intent of the authors. Every effort has been made to trace the owners of copyrighted material.

Cover photograph courtesy The Library of Congress.

LIBRARY OF CONGRESS CATALOGING-IN-PUBLICATION DATA

Amendment XIX : granting women the right to vote / Carrie Fredericks, book editor.
    p. cm. -- (Constitutional amendments: beyond the Bill of Rights)
    Includes bibliographical references and index.
    ISBN 978-0-7377-4127-8 (hardcover)
    1. Women--Suffrage--United States--History. 2. United States. Constitution. 19th Amendment--History. 3. Women--Suffrage--United States. I. Fredericks, Carrie. II. Title: Amendment 19. III. Title: Amendment nineteen. IV. Title: Granting women the right to vote.
    KF4895.A954 2009
    342.73'072--dc22

                                                                    2008045046

Printed in the United States of America
1 2 3 4 5 6 7 13 12 11 10 09

Contents

Chapter 1: Historical Background on the Nineteenth Amendment

Chapter 2: Voting Rights Trials

Appendices

Granting Women the Right to Vote

> "Today's Constitution is a realistic document of freedom only because of several corrective amendments. Those amendments speak to a sense of decency and fairness."
>
> Thurgood Marshall

While the U.S. Constitution forms the backbone of American democracy, the amendments make the Constitution a living, ever-evolving document. Interpretation and analysis of the Constitution inform lively debate in every branch of government, as well as among students, scholars, and all other citizens, and views on various articles of the Constitution have changed over the generations. Formally altering the Constitution, however, can happen only through the amendment process. The Greenhaven Press series The Bill of Rights examines the first ten amendments to the Constitution. Constitutional Amendments: Beyond the Bill of Rights continues the exploration, addressing key amendments ratified since 1791.

The process of amending the Constitution is painstaking. While other options are available, the method used for nearly every amendment begins with a congressional bill that must pass both the Senate and the House of Representatives by a two-thirds majority. Then the amendment must be ratified by three-quarters of the states. Many amendments have been proposed since the Bill of Rights was adopted in 1791, but only seventeen have been ratified.

It may be difficult to imagine a United States where women and African Americans are prohibited from voting, where the

9

federal government allows one human being to enslave another, or where some citizens are denied equal protection under the law. While many of our most fundamental liberties are protected by the Bill of Rights, the amendments that followed have significantly broadened and enhanced the rights of American citizens. Such rights may be taken for granted today, but when the amendments were ratified, many were considered groundbreaking and proved to be explosively controversial.

Each volume in Constitutional Amendments provides an in-depth exploration of an amendment and its impact through primary and secondary sources, both historical and contemporary. Primary sources include landmark Supreme Court rulings, speeches by prominent experts, and newspaper editorials. Secondary sources include historical analyses, law journal articles, book excerpts, and magazine articles. Each volume first presents the historical background of the amendment, creating a colorful picture of the circumstances surrounding the amendment's passage: the campaigns to sway public opinion, the congressional debates, and the struggle for ratification. Next, each volume examines the ways the court system has been used to test the validity of the amendment and addresses the ramifications of the amendment's passage. The final chapter of each volume presents viewpoints that explore current controversies and debates relating to ways in which the amendment affects our everyday lives.

Numerous features are included in each Constitutional Amendments volume:

- An originally written introduction presents a concise yet thorough overview of the amendment.

- A time line provides historical context by describing key events, organizations, and people relating to the ratification of the amendment, subsequent court cases, and the impact of the amendment.

- An annotated table of contents offers an at-a-glance summary of each primary and secondary source essay included in the volume.

- The complete text of the amendment, followed by a "plain English" explanation, brings the amendment into clear focus for students and other readers.

- Graphs, charts, tables, and maps enhance the text.

- A list of all twenty-seven Constitutional Amendments offers quick reference.

- An annotated list of court cases relevant to the amendment broadens the reader's understanding of the judiciary's role in interpreting the Constitution.

- A bibliography of books, periodicals, and Web sites aids readers in further research.

- A detailed subject index allows readers to quickly find the information they need.

With the aid of this series, students and other researchers will become better informed of their rights and responsibilities as American citizens. Constitutional Amendments: Beyond the Bill of Rights examines the roots of American democracy, bringing to life the ways the Constitution has evolved and how it has impacted this nation's history.

Amendment Text and Explanation

The Nineteenth Amendment to the U.S. Constitution

Section 1. The right of the citizens of the United States to vote shall not be denied or abridged by the United States or by any State on account of sex.

Section 2. Congress shall have power to enforce this article by appropriate legislation.

Explanation

The first section of the Nineteenth Amendment guarantees that any citizen of the United States can vote, regardless of whether the individual is male or female. The second section of the amendment states that the U.S. Congress has the authority to pass laws to make sure the amendment is upheld.

Passed by Congress June 4, 1919. Ratified August 18, 1920.

Introduction

In the twenty-first century, a woman's right to vote is taken for granted. For modern American women, the idea of being denied the right to vote because of gender is ridiculous, but less than a hundred years ago, women were not permitted to vote in most states. It was a long, difficult struggle to attain this basic right.

In the decades leading up to the passage of the Nineteenth Amendment to the U.S. Constitution, many considered the prospect of women's suffrage ludicrous. Women, seen as weaker in mind and incapable of making complex decisions, had few rights in any aspect of their lives. Husbands, fathers, or brothers controlled the wages that women earned, as well as their land, property, and persons. No woman was allowed to be truly independent of men.

Many men feared that allowing women to vote would fundamentally alter the gender-based hierarchy and destroy the American family. In 1920 antisuffragist Isaac Lockhart Peebles claimed that women's suffrage aimed not just to make women equal with men but to make them the rulers of men. In this context, the right to vote was about much more than just having a voice in the political process: It was about women's independence and ability to think and act for themselves, as well as a challenge to the notion that men should have total control over women.

When the United States of America was formed, women had no place in the legal system. The new Constitution did not refer to women or to any rights pertaining to them, and most states followed suit. New Jersey was the exception. In its new constitution, the state gave voting rights to all free residents meeting the voting criteria. This suffrage was to be short-lived, though; the right was repealed in 1807.

In the United States the notion of women's suffrage originated in Puritan New England. One of the most outspoken women of the 1600s was Anne Hutchinson of Massachusetts; she advocated for women's right to decide for themselves how different aspects of the community would affect them. Hutchinson was a charismatic speaker, and more and more people, both men and women, began to listen to her. This troubled the men ruling the colony, and she was subsequently charged with religious crimes and banished. When she left Massachusetts, more than thirty families followed her.

The first half of the nineteenth century saw more women begin to argue for suffrage. Women were speaking up about their status, both in society and in the law. Several girls' schools and academies opened during this time. In an 1820 letter, Frances Wright wrote about the education of females: "In a country where a mother is charged with the formation of an infant mind that is to be called in future to judge of the laws and support the liberties of a republic, the mother herself should well understand those laws and estimate those liberties."

Also at this time, many women became involved in the fight to end slavery, a cause that led naturally to women's suffrage. In 1840 Lucretia Mott and Elizabeth Cady Stanton attended an antislavery conference in London, but they were not allowed to participate because of their gender. They returned to the United States strongly motivated to solidify a women's rights movement. Eight years later, they held a women's rights convention in Seneca Falls, New York, that became known the world over. Convention attendees drafted the Declaration of Sentiments, a document modeled on the Declaration on Independence, proclaiming the rights of women: "We hold these truths to be self-evident, that all men and women are created equal."

The right to vote was not embraced by all of the women at this first convention. Lucretia Mott and Elizabeth Cady

Stanton differed in their opinions on the matter. Mott did not want voting rights to be included in the Declaration, fearing that the idea of women's suffrage would draw attention away from other rights that were being declared. Stanton persevered, though, and on this issue, the Declaration of Sentiments finally stated "that it is the duty of women of this country to secure to themselves their sacred right to the elective franchise."

In many newspapers the convention was vilified, reflecting the widespread belief that the notion of women's rights was at best comical and at worst dangerous. Only a small number of papers supported the gathering, including the abolitionist paper *The North Star*, founded by Frederick Douglass. Douglass remarked on those who opposed rights for women: "A discussion of the rights of animals would be regarded with far more complacency by many of what are called the 'wise' and the 'good' of our land, than would a discussion of the rights of women. It is, in their estimation, to be guilty of evil thoughts, to think that woman is entitled to equal rights with man."

Over the next two decades women fought for both suffrage and abolitionism. During the American Civil War, women's issues took a backseat to the antislavery cause. After the war, the American Equal Rights Association was formed, bringing together advocates of both causes to focus on achieving voting rights for blacks and for women. During the Reconstruction period following the Civil War, the main objective of political maneuvering was to get former slaves the right to vote, but many women hoped to have women's suffrage included as part of the Reconstruction program as well. In an 1865 letter, suffragist Elizabeth Cady Stanton wrote, "If our rulers have the justice to give the black man suffrage, woman should avail herself of this newborn virtue and secure her rights. If not, she should begin with renewed earnestness to educate the people into the idea of true universal suffrage."

After the Fourteenth Amendment passed with no language specifying rights for women, a schism occurred in the ranks of the suffragists, who disagreed over the best method of furthering their agenda. In 1869 Susan B. Anthony and Elizabeth Cady Stanton formed the National Woman Suffrage Association (NWSA). Another group, the American Woman Suffrage Association (AWSA), was formed by Lucy Stone. The AWSA focused on securing voting rights on a state-by-state basis, while the NWSA proposed a national referendum on the issue.

As these two groups established themselves, the right to vote was granted to women in several western states. In 1869 and 1870, respectively, Wyoming and Utah granted women voting rights, and in the 1890s two more western states, Colorado and Idaho, followed suit.

Elsewhere in the country, the fight for women's suffrage led to arrests on several occasions. When Susan B. Anthony was arrested in 1872 for actually casting a vote in that year's presidential election, she used her arrest as a rallying cry for her cause. When she was found guilty of voting illegally, Anthony stated to the courtroom, "Your denial of my citizen's right to vote, is the denial of my right of consent as one of the governed, the denial of my right of representation as one of the taxed, the denial of my right to a trial by jury of my peers as an offender against law, therefore, the denial of my sacred rights to life, liberty, property."

The decade before the turn of the century saw the two leading suffrage groups merge back into one, allowing the new organization to harness all available resources to continue the suffrage fight. A new generation of women began to lead the suffragists. By 1900 most of the early suffragists had died. The movement's new leaders—Carrie Chapman Catt, Harriot Stanton Blatch, Alice Paul, and others—were making names for themselves in the suffrage world.

Alice Paul did much to further the cause. By picketing outside the White House with other women, Paul made it almost impossible for politicians to ignore the issues put before them. When many of the protesters were arrested and charged with obstructing traffic, women's suffrage became even harder to ignore. These women were beaten, knocked unconscious, and given food infested with worms. When word of their treatment reached the press, Congress was still moving extremely slowly on the suffrage issue. Even though both the House of Representatives and the Senate had set up committees to study women's suffrage in the 1880s, it would be many more years before the Nineteenth Amendment was passed.

Many states, though, were taking care of the matter themselves. California, Kansas, Oregon, Arizona, New York, Oklahoma, and South Dakota joined the four western states that had granted full suffrage to women.

When the Nineteenth Amendment was finally passed, women and their supporters all over the country celebrated. In a telegram to Carrie Chapman Catt, President Woodrow Wilson wrote, "I join with you and all friends of the suffrage cause in rejoicing over the adoption of the suffrage amendment by the Congress. Please accept and convey to your association my warmest congratulations."

After the Nineteenth Amendment was ratified by the required thirty-six states, it was adopted as part of the Constitution. The amendment gave voting rights to all female citizens: any woman in any town in any state in the country. The number of voters jumped dramatically, though not all women took advantage of the opportunity to vote.

After the amendment's passage, many people believed that the fight for women's rights was over. But that was far from true, and in an effort to expand women's rights, another amendment was soon proposed: On the seventy-fifth anniversary of the Seneca Falls Convention, only three years after the Nineteenth Amendment was ratified, Alice Paul proposed the

Equal Rights Amendment to address other equally important aspects of women's rights. In Paul's view, winning the right to vote did not mean the fight was over. This amendment passed Congress but never attained ratification by the required number of states. Some fifty years later, the Equal Rights Amendment became a rallying cry for an entirely new generation of American women during the socially and politically turbulent time of the late 1960s and 1970s.

In a 1972 interview, Alice Paul discussed her place in American history and her fight for the rights enjoyed by so many women: "I never doubted that equal rights was the right direction. Most reforms, most problems are complicated. But to me there is nothing complicated about ordinary equality."

Even though suffrage has been a right of women for some ninety years, some persist in believing that women should not have the right to vote. In 2001 a Kansas state senator stated publicly that women should not vote. Senator Kay O'Connor spoke with the *Kansas City Star*, saying, "I'm an old fashioned woman. Men should take care of women, and if men were taking care of women we wouldn't have to vote." According to a 2001 Associated Press report, Senator O'Connor believed the Nineteenth Amendment was responsible for putting women into the workplace and taking them out of the home.

In a 2007 interview with the *New York Observer*, conservative author Ann Coulter stated, "If we took away women's right to vote we would never have to worry about another Democratic president. It's kind of a pipe dream, it's a personal fantasy of mine, but I don't think its going to happen. And it is a good way of making the point that women are voting so stupidly, at least single women."

These views are in direct contrast with an editorial written by Arthur Brisbane in the Hearst Newspapers around 1917. Brisbane wrote, "The woman who votes becomes an important factor in life, for a double reason. In the first place, when a woman votes the candidate must take care that his conduct and record meet with a good woman's approval, and this makes better men of the candidates."

The Nineteenth Amendment was about so much more than just votes for women. Education, the freedom to make choices for themselves, and the ability to lead independent lives were just a few of the important issues that went along with women's suffrage. The Nineteenth Amendment allowed women to take their place in the political arena and to influence the laws affecting their daily lives.

Chronology

1634
After leaving England to escape religious persecution, Anne Hutchinson and her family settle in Massachusetts. She holds regular meetings for women and raises the issue of women's rights. Although she gains many followers, the strict Puritan leadership of the Massachusetts Bay Colony persecutes and eventually banishes her from the community.

1777
Abigail Adams, the wife of John Adams, a member of the Continental Congress and later U.S. president, asks her husband to take into account the concerns of women when putting together the U.S. Constitution. She contends that women should not be entirely dependent on the whims of their husbands and fathers.

1790
New Jersey gives the right to vote to all free inhabitants of the colony.

1807
New Jersey repeals voting rights for women.

1833
Oberlin College in Ohio becomes the first college to admit both men and women.

1837
The first college for women, Mount Holyoke, is founded in South Hadley, Massachusetts.

1840
An antislavery convention is held in London, England. Lucretia Mott and Elizabeth Cady Stanton attend the convention, but they are barred from participating because they are wo-

men. The experience prompts them to organize a women's rights convention in the United States.

1848

In July a groundbreaking women's rights convention is held in Seneca Falls, New York, brought together by Lucretia Mott and Elizabeth Cady Stanton. Suffrage for women is discussed and the Declaration of Sentiments, a document modeled on the Declaration of Independence that calls for acknowledgment of the rights of women, is presented. In August another session is held in Rochester, New York.

1849

Elizabeth Blackwell becomes the first woman to be awarded a medical degree in the United States. She graduates from Geneva College in New York.

1850

The first National Women's Rights Convention is held in Worcester, Massachusetts, in October of this year.

1851

Elizabeth Cady Stanton and Susan B. Anthony meet. This is the beginning of a fifty-year friendship and partnership working for voting, economic, and legal rights for women. Another women's rights convention is held in Akron, Ohio, at which Sojourner Truth gives her famous "Ain't I a Woman?" speech.

1853

Suffragists hold a meeting in New York City during the World's Fair. This gathering soon becomes known as "The Mob Convention" because of the protests that occur. Annual women's rights conventions are now being held. They will continue until the start of the Civil War. During wartime, work on women's suffrage stops almost entirely because women are aiding the war effort.

1866

The American Equal Rights Association is formed, bringing together suffragists and antislavery advocates. Congress passes the Fourteenth Amendment, which defines citizens of the United States as male.

1868

The Fourteenth Amendment is ratified. Susan B. Anthony and Elizabeth Cady Stanton begin publishing *The Revolution*, a weekly newspaper supporting women's suffrage.

1869

The Fifteenth Amendment, giving black males the right to vote, is passed by Congress on February 26, 1869. The women's suffrage movement experiences growing pains. During this time many important people, such as Frederick Douglass, who had previously supported women's suffrage, now turn their attention to black male suffrage. This leads to a split in the women's suffrage movement: Elizabeth Cady Stanton forms the National Woman Suffrage Association with Susan B. Anthony and becomes the organization's president, while Lucy Stone forms the American Woman Suffrage Association with Henry Ward Beecher as president. A bright spot for suffragists is the granting of voting rights to women by the state of Wyoming.

1870

Utah follows Wyoming in granting suffrage to women. The Fifteenth Amendment is ratified. The ratification of this amendment leads women in Massachusetts to try to vote; they are unsuccessful.

1872–1873

In November 1872 Susan B. Anthony and several other women are arrested for illegal voting. In 1873 Anthony is tried and found guilty. She uses her arrest as a way to bring greater attention to women's suffrage.

1874

The Supreme Court takes up the issue of women's suffrage. In *Minor v. Happersett*, the Court rules that suffrage is not among the "privileges and immunities" guaranteed by the Constitution.

1875

Michigan and Minnesota grant voting rights to women for school elections.

1880

Lucretia Mott dies. After organizing the Seneca Falls Convention with Elizabeth Cady Stanton in 1848, Mott spent many years traveling the country and advocating for the rights of women and blacks.

1882

The U.S. House of Representatives and Senate appoint committees to study women's suffrage. The branches of Congress will debate this issue in the coming years.

1883

Washington Territory grants full voting rights to women.

1887

Washington Territory's women's suffrage law is struck down. Women lose the right to vote in Utah through congressional action.

1890

After the setbacks of the late 1880s, the two leading women's suffrage groups merge, becoming the National American Woman Suffrage Association. Elizabeth Cady Stanton is named the organization's president.

1893

Colorado gives women the right to vote. Carrie Chapman Catt is instrumental in this effort.

1896
Utah becomes a state and women regain their right to vote. Idaho grants women the right to vote.

1900
Carrie Chapman Catt succeeds Susan B. Anthony as president of the National American Woman Suffrage Association, signaling the beginning of a new generation of women leading the fight for national suffrage.

1902
Elizabeth Cady Stanton dies. Although Stanton had started out as an abolitionist, she later turned her focus to women's rights. For decades she worked tirelessly for the cause of women's suffrage and equal rights and was known for criticizing religion as an oppressor of women. She famously stated, "We are the only class in history that has been left to fight its battles alone, unaided by the ruling powers. White labor and the freed black men had their champions, but where are ours?"

1906
Susan B. Anthony, the most famous suffragist, dies. The Nineteenth Amendment is often referred to as the Susan B. Anthony Amendment. Throughout her life, Anthony was a strong supporter of all rights for women, including voting, economic, and social rights. She saw women's suffrage as an important way to achieve equal status under the law.

1907
Elizabeth Cady Stanton's daughter, Harriot Stanton Blatch, forms the Equality League of Self Supporting Women in 1907. This group's aim is to further the independence of women in political and social arenas.

1910
The Equality League of Self Supporting Women becomes the Women's Political Union and holds its first suffrage parade in New York City.

1911

California grants voting rights to women. The National Association Opposed to Woman Suffrage is founded. This group is dedicated to repealing the voting rights of women and making sure that a national referendum is not carried out.

1912

Kansas, Oregon, and Arizona grant voting rights to women.

1915

Carrie Chapman Catt again becomes president of the National American Woman Suffrage Association. She focuses her campaign for voting rights on the states rather than pursuing a national referendum.

1916

There is discontent among the suffragists. Alice Paul leaves the National American Woman Suffrage Association to form the National Woman's Party. Although she agrees with Carrie Chapman Catt on the need for women's suffrage, Paul holds a different view on how to bring this about.

1917

Alice Paul and members of the National Woman's Party picket outside the White House. Many of the women are arrested and charged with obstructing traffic. These arrests will later be ruled illegal. Women win the right to vote in presidential elections in Indiana, Michigan, Nebraska, and North Dakota. New York, Oklahoma, and South Dakota grant full suffrage.

1919

On June 4, the Nineteenth Amendment is passed by the U.S. Congress.

1920

The Nineteenth Amendment is ratified by the last of the required thirty-six states. It is adopted as part of the U.S. Constitution on August 26, 1920.

1923

Marking the seventy-fifth anniversary of the Seneca Falls Convention, Alice Paul proposes the Equal Rights Amendment to address inadequacies in the Nineteenth Amendment.

1971

The voting age in the United States is lowered to eighteen.

1972

After almost fifty years, the Equal Rights Amendment is passed by both houses of Congress and signed by President Richard M. Nixon. The deadline for state ratification is extended to 1982, but the amendment falls short by three states. It is not adopted but has come before every session of Congress since then.

Historical Background on the Nineteenth Amendment

The Seneca Falls Convention

Frederick Douglass

On July 28, 1848, Frederick Douglass published an editorial in The North Star *on the Women's Rights Convention held that month in Seneca Falls, New York. Douglass describes the women's "marked ability and dignity." He notes that several important documents on women's rights were put forth, notably the Declaration of Sentiments, and goes on to discuss the rights of women. He offers his support for the convention by declaring that women are entitled to all the rights enjoyed by men. Douglass, a former slave who became a world-famous speaker, author, and abolitionist, founded the newspaper* The North Star *in Rochester, New York, publishing the first edition on December 3, 1847.*

One of the most interesting events of the past week, was the holding of what is technically styled a Woman's Rights Convention at Seneca Falls. The speaking, addresses, and resolutions of this extraordinary meeting was wholly conducted by women; and although they evidently felt themselves in a novel position, it is but simple justice to say that their whole proceedings were characterized by marked ability and dignity. No one present, we think, however much he might be disposed to differ from the views advanced by the leading speakers on that occasion, will fail to give them credit for brilliant talents and excellent dispositions. In this meeting, as in other deliberative assemblies, there were frequent differences of opinion and animated discussion; but in no case was there the slightest absence of good feeling and decorum. Several interesting documents setting forth the rights as well as the grievances of women were read. Among these was a Declaration of Sentiments, to be regarded as the basis of a grand movement for attaining the civil, social, political, and religious rights of women.

Frederick Douglass, "The Rights of Women," *The North Star*, Rochester, NY, July 28, 1848.

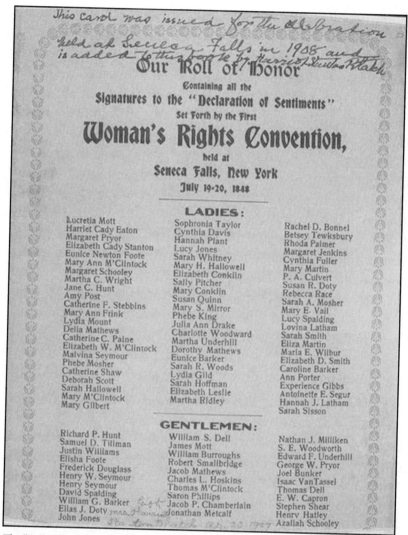

This card was issued for the celebration held at Seneca Falls in 1908 and is added to this book by Harriot Stanton Blatch

Our Roll of Honor

Containing all the
Signatures to the "Declaration of Sentiments"
Set Forth by the First

Woman's Rights Convention,

held at
Seneca Falls, New York
July 19-20, 1848

LADIES:

Lucretia Mott
Harriet Cady Eaton
Margaret Pryor
Elizabeth Cady Stanton
Eunice Newton Foote
Mary Ann M'Clintock
Margaret Schooley
Martha C. Wright
Jane C. Hunt
Amy Post
Catherine F. Stebbins
Mary Ann Frink
Lydia Mount
Delia Mathews
Catherine C. Paine
Elizabeth W. M'Clintock
Malvina Seymour
Phebe Mosher
Catherine Shaw
Deborah Scott
Sarah Hallowell
Mary M'Clintock
Mary Gilbert

Sophronia Taylor
Cynthia Davis
Hannah Plant
Lucy Jones
Sarah Whitney
Mary H. Hallowell
Elizabeth Conklin
Sally Pitcher
Mary Conklin
Susan Quinn
Mary S. Mirror
Phebe King
Julia Ann Drake
Charlotte Woodward
Martha Underhill
Dorothy Mathews
Eunice Barker
Sarah R. Woods
Lydia Gild
Sarah Hoffman
Elizabeth Leslie
Martha Ridley

Rachel D. Bonnel
Betsey Tewksbury
Rhoda Palmer
Margaret Jenkins
Cynthia Fuller
Mary Martin
P. A. Culvert
Susan R. Doty
Rebecca Race
Sarah A. Mosher
Mary E. Vail
Lucy Spalding
Lovina Latham
Sarah Smith
Eliza Martin
Maria E. Wilbur
Elizabeth D. Smith
Caroline Barker
Ann Porter
Experience Gibbs
Antoinette E. Segur
Hannah J. Latham
Sarah Sisson

GENTLEMEN:

Richard P. Hunt
Samuel D. Tillman
Justin Williams
Elisha Foote
Frederick Douglass
Henry W. Seymour
Henry Seymour
David Spalding
William G. Barker
Elias J. Doty
John Jones

William S. Dell
James Mott
William Burroughs
Robert Smallbridge
Jacob Mathews
Charles L. Hoskins
Thomas M'Clintock
Saron Phillips
Jacob P. Chamberlain
Jonathan Metcalf

Nathan J. Milliken
S. E. Woodworth
Edward F. Underhill
George W. Pryor
Joel Bunker
Isaac VanTassel
Thomas Dell
E. W. Capron
Stephen Shear
Henry Hatley
Azaliah Schooley

The "Roll of Honor,"—signatures to the Declaration of Sentiments set forth at the First Women's Convention in Seneca Falls, New York, in 1848. The Library of Congress.

We should not do justice to our own convictions, or to the excellent persons connected with this infant movement, if we did not in this connection offer a few remarks on the general subject which the Convention met to consider and the objects they seek to attain.

In doing so, we are not insensible that the bare mention of this truly important subject in any other than terms of contemptuous ridicule and scornful disfavor, is likely to excite against us the fury of bigotry and the folly of prejudice. A discussion of the rights of animals would be regarded with far more complacency by many of what are called the "wise" and the "good" of our land, than would a discussion of the rights of women. It is, in their estimation to be guilty of evil thoughts, to think that woman is entitled to equal rights with man. Many who have at last made the discovery that the negroes have some rights as well as other members of the human family, have yet to be convinced that women are entitled to any. Eight years ago a number of persons of this description actually abandoned the anti-slavery cause, lest by giving their influence in that direction they might possibly be giving countenance to the dangerous heresy that woman, in respect to rights, stands on an equal footing with man. In the judgment of such persons the American slave system, with all its concomitant horrors, is less to be deplored than this "wicked" idea. It is perhaps needless to say, that we cherish little sympathy for such sentiments or respect for such prejudices.

Standing as we do up on the watch-tower of human freedom, we cannot be deterred from an expression of our approbation of any movement, however humble, to improve and elevate the character of any members of the human family. While it is impossible for us to go into this subject at length, and dispose of the various objections which are often urged against such a doctrine as that of female equality, we are free to say that in respect to political rights, we hold woman to be justly entitled to all we claim for man. We go farther, and express our conviction that all political rights which it is expedient for man to exercise, it is equally for woman. All that distinguishes man as an intelligent and accountable being, is equally true of woman, and if that government only is just which governs by the free consent of the governed, there can be no reason in the world for denying to woman the exercise of the elective franchise, or a hand in making and administering the laws of the land. Our doctrine is that "right is of no sex." We therefore bid the women engaged in this movement our humble Godspeed.

Post–Civil War Struggles

Ellen DuBois

In the following selection, Ellen DuBois discusses the women's rights movement following the Civil War. Before the war, the movement had focused more on women's economic rights than on voting rights. But after the war, the rights of women became linked with the rights of former slaves. As DuBois notes, women objected strongly to the wording of the Fourteenth Amendment to the U.S. Constitution, which granted former slaves the right to vote but limited that right to men. In 1869 the women's movement split into two groups with very different strategies on how to obtain the vote for women, one focusing on attaining a federal women's suffrage amendment, and the other pursuing individual state amendments. The article concludes by considering the legacy of the Reconstruction era for the women's movement. DuBois is a professor of history at the University of California, Los Angeles.

The origins of the American women's suffrage movement are commonly dated from the public protest meeting, held in Seneca Falls, New York, in July 1848. At that historic meeting, the right of women to join with men in the privileges and obligations of active, voting citizenship was the one demand that raised eyebrows among the 100 or so women and men attending. As Elizabeth Cady Stanton, the meeting's prime organizer, remembered it, many in the audience, even including the distinguished radical Lucretia Mott, worried that the demand for political equality was either too advanced or too morally questionable to include on the launching platform of the new movement. Joined only by abolitionist and ex-slave Frederick Douglass, Stanton argued for the importance of women's equal participation in the electoral process.

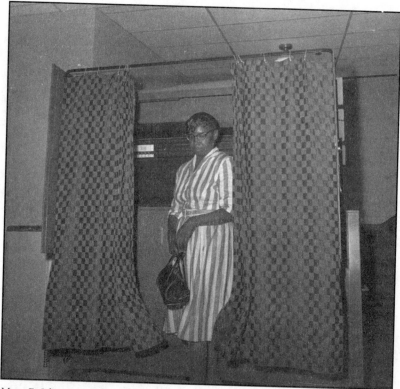

Mary E. Johnson, a black woman, casts a vote at the polls in Louisiana in 1962. AP Images.

In the end, the suffrage resolution passed, the only one of the meeting's thirteen demands not to be unanimously embraced. From that point it was another three-quarters of a century to the 1920 ratification of the nineteenth constitutional amendment, which prohibited the states from "disfranchisement on the basis of sex."

Given the seventy-two years between the one event and the other, a full third of our history as a nation, the story of the demand for equal suffrage involves many stops and starts, and numerous shifts and splits. Moreover, the exact terms and times of the triumphant end were not—and could not have been—envisioned by those present at the beginning. Differences in and conflicts over leadership, shifting political environments, and various strategies and tactics all mark the long and complex history of the women's suffrage movement, which lasted far longer than its instigators imagined and yet was shorter than it could have been (when we consider, for instance, the additional three and a half decades that elapsed before women won the right to vote in that other eighteenth-century revolutionary nation, France).

Voting Is Not the Primary Goal

This essay will consider the impact of the Civil War and Reconstruction epoch on the American battle for women's suffrage. As of 1860, the right to vote was not the primary demand of the women's rights movement, which focused much more on the economic rights of women—and especially of wives—to earn, inherit, and hold property. In addition, because the common reading of the federal Constitution was that it was up to the separate states to determine how to establish the electorate, women's rights activists assumed that women's suffrage—along with women's economic and other rights—had to be fought for and won state by state. Thus, it was not anticipated that winning the right to vote would involve an epic battle over the federal Constitution. We should remember that as of 1860, only twelve amendments—ten of them consisting of the Bill of Rights dating from 1787, and the other two of largely procedural significance—had been ratified. What we know now—that the history of American federal constitutionalism would be marked by alternating periods of interpretation and amendment, of fierce battles waged far beyond Congress and the Supreme Court to alter and augment the shape and meaning of our foundational political document—was not obvious then; nor was it obvious that women's suffrage would be the most prolonged of all these constitutional wars.

Women and Slaves Are Linked Together

The very first of those periods of constitutional struggle occurred during the era of postwar Reconstruction, which is when the women's suffrage movement took on many of the characteristics that it was to maintain for the next half century. Emerging out of the Civil War, the issue of political equality for women was inextricably bound up with the unsettled political status of the former slaves. When the Thirteenth Amendment passed Congress (with the help of a massive petition campaign engineered by the women's rights movement) and was ratified by the states [in 1865], the former slaves were freed, but the absence of chattel slavery did not specify what the presence of freedom meant legally and constitutionally. To resolve the anomalous position of the freed population, the Fourteenth Amendment [ratified in 1868] declared that "all persons born or naturalized in the United States were citizens thereof," with all the "privileges and immunities" of national citizenship. Without specifying exactly what these privileges and immunities were, the second section of the amendment went on to address the crucial question of voting rights for the freedmen, a question of particular concern to the ruling Republican party, which looked to them as a loyal constituency in the states of the former Confederacy.

The Fourteenth Amendment addressed the question of enfranchisement in an indirect, elaborate, and ultimately ineffective way: by pinning a state's number of seats in the House of Representatives to the proportion of the adult population that was permitted to vote. There were, however, two qualifications to this population basis for determining representation: "Indians not taxed" were excluded, and the amendment specifically defined the potential electorate as "male." Here, for the first time, was an explicit reference to gender in the U.S. Constitution. Since the women's rights movement was now in its second decade and included a call for political equality in its platform, the amenders of the Constitution could no longer assume, as had the Founders, that "we the people" simply meant men, and did not include, in any politically significant way, women. Women had to be explicitly excluded or they would be implicitly included.

Objections to the Fourteenth Amendment

Women's rights activists objected strongly to what Elizabeth Cady Stanton angrily called "that word 'male.'" They sent petitions to Congress while the amendment was still being drafted, begging for a change in language, but the amendment passed Congress and was sent to the states for ratification with the disturbing qualification of gender intact within it. Women's rights activists objected and criticized, but were caught between their recognition of the importance of political rights for the freedmen and their dedication to their own cause of women's rights. So they stopped short of calling for non-ratification of the Fourteenth Amendment.

Later, because the measures used in the Fourteenth Amendment to encourage black enfranchisement were too weak, a third postwar amendment was designed, this time to address the issue of suffrage directly. The Fifteenth Amendment, passed by Congress in 1869 and ratified two years later, explicitly forbade the states to deny the right to vote to anyone on the basis of "race, color or previous condition of servitude" and authorized Congress to pass any necessary enforcement legislation. The wording, it should be noted, did not transfer the right to determine the electorate to the federal government, but only specified particular kinds of state disfranchisements—and "sex" was not one of them—as unconstitutional.

Antagonism Between the Movements

At this point, the delicate balance between the political agendas of the causes of black freedom and women's rights became undone. The two movements came into open antagonism, and the women's rights movement itself split over the next steps to take to secure women the right to vote. Defenders of women's rights found themselves in an extremely difficult political quandary. Would they have to oppose an advance in the rights of the ex-slaves in order to argue for those of free women? At a May 1869 meeting of the American Equal Rights Association, a group that had been organized three years earlier by women's rights advocates to link black and woman suffrage, Elizabeth Cady Stanton gave vent to her frustration, her sense of betrayal by longstanding male allies, and her underlying sense that "educated" women like herself were more worthy of enfranchisement than men just emerged from slavery. She and Frederick Douglass had a painful and famous public exchange about the relative importance of black and women's suffrage, in which Douglass invoked images of ex-slaves "hung from lampposts" in the South by white supremacist vigilantes, and Stanton retaliated by asking whether he thought that the black race was made up only and entirely of men. By the end of the meeting, Stanton and her partner Susan B. Anthony had led a walkout of a portion of the women at the meeting to form a new organization to focus on women's suffrage, which they named the National Woman Suffrage Association.

Two Groups, Two Strategies

A second group, under the leadership of Massachusetts women Lucy Stone and Julia Ward Howe, formed a rival organization, known as the American Woman Suffrage Association. This wing counted on longstanding connections with abolitionism and the leadership of the Republican Party to get women's suffrage enacted once black male suffrage had been fully inscribed in the Constitution. Over the next few years, both the American and the National Woman Suffrage Associations spread their influence to the Midwest and the Pacific Coast.

The National Woman Suffrage Association linked political rights to other causes, including inflammatory ones like free love, while the American Woman Suffrage Association kept the issue clear of "side issues." For the next few years, the two organizations pursued different strategies to secure votes for women. Starting with an 1874 campaign in Michigan, the American Woman Suffrage Association pressed for changes in state constitutions. Because these campaigns involved winning over a majority of (male) voters, they were extremely difficult to carry out, and it was not until 1893 that Colorado became the first state to enfranchise women.

Meanwhile, the National Woman Suffrage Association refused to give up on the national Constitution. Doubtful that any additional federal amendments would be passed, the group sought a way to base women's suffrage in the Constitution's existing provisions. Its "New Departure" campaign contended that the Fourteenth Amendment's assertion that all native-born or naturalized "persons" were national citizens surely included the right of suffrage among its "privileges and immunities," and that, as persons, women were thus enfranchised. In 1871, the notorious female radical Victoria Woodhull made this argument before the House Judiciary Committee. The next year, hundreds of suffragists around the country went to the polls on election day, repeating the arguments of the New Departure, and pressing to get their votes accepted.

Minor v. Happersett

Among those who succeeded—at least temporarily—was Susan B. Anthony, who cast her ballot for Ulysses S. Grant. Three weeks after the election, Anthony was arrested on federal charges of "illegal voting" and in 1873 was found guilty by an all-male jury. Anthony was prevented by the judge from appealing her case but another "voting woman," Virginia Minor, succeeded in making the New Departure argument before the U.S. Supreme Court in 1874. In a landmark voting and women's rights decision, the Court ruled that although women were indeed persons, and hence citizens, the case failed because suffrage was not included in the rights guaranteed by that status. The 1875 *Minor vs. Happersett* ruling coincided with other decisions that allowed states to infringe on the voting rights of the Southern freedmen, culminating over the next two decades in their near-total disfranchisement.

The Reconstruction Legacy

Although these various Reconstruction-era efforts failed to enfranchise women, they did leave various marks on the continuing campaign for women's suffrage: a shifting focus on state and federal constitutional action, a legacy of direct action, a women's suffrage movement that was largely cut off from the efforts of African Americans for their rights, and, perhaps most fundamentally, an independent movement of women for women, which turned the campaign for suffrage into a continuing source of activism and political sophistication for coming generations of women.

The Resignation of a Legend

Elizabeth Cady Stanton

The following selection presents in full "The Solitude of Self," the speech that Elizabeth Cady Stanton delivered in January 1892 upon her resignation as president of the National Woman Suffrage Association. Stanton subsequently delivered this speech to the U.S. House Committee on the Judiciary and to the Senate Committee on Woman Suffrage. In her diary, she wrote that the speech was "the best thing I have ever written." In it she argues for the need for all human beings, both men and women, to develop fully as individuals—that is, to pursue a complete education and to develop the skills necessary for self-sufficiency. Stanton points out that, ultimately, everyone must rely on his or her own resources; regardless of one's circumstances, she writes, "each soul must depend wholly on itself." She asserts that no person can take on the rights and responsibilities of another, and therefore all individuals must be endowed with full political, religious, and social rights. Stanton formed the National Woman Suffrage Association in 1869 with Susan B. Anthony. She was an instrumental force in the first fifty years of the women's suffrage movement.

The point I wish plainly to bring before you on this occasion is the individuality of each human soul; our Protestant idea, the right of individual conscience and judgment—our republican idea, individual citizenship. In discussing the rights of woman, we are to consider, first, what belongs to her as an individual, in a world of her own, the arbiter of her own destiny, an imaginary Robinson Crusoe with her woman Friday on a solitary island. Her rights under such circumstances are to use all her faculties for her own safety and happiness.

Elizabeth Cady Stanton, "The Solitude of Self," Hearing of the Woman Suffrage Association before the U.S. Committee on the Judiciary, January 18, 1892. www.loc.gov.

Secondly, if we consider her as a citizen, as a member of a great nation, she must have the same rights as all other members, according to the fundamental principles of our Government.

Thirdly, viewed as a woman, an equal factor in civilization, her rights and duties are still the same—individual happiness and development.

Fourthly, it is only the incidental relations of life, such as mother, wife, sister, daughter, that may involve some special duties and training. In the usual discussion in regard to woman's sphere, such men as Herbert Spencer, Frederic Harrison, and Grant Allen uniformly subordinate her rights and duties as an individual, as a citizen, as a woman, to the necessities of these incidental relations, some of which a large class of women may never assume. In discussing the sphere of man we do not decide his rights as an individual, as a citizen, as a man by his duties as a father, a husband, a brother, or a son, relations some of which he may never still. Moreover he would be better fitted for these very relations and whatever special work he might choose to do to earn his bread by the complete development of all his faculties as an individual.

Education for Women

Just so with woman. The education that will fit her to discharge the duties in the largest sphere of human usefulness will best fit her for whatever special work she may be compelled to do.

The isolation of every human soul and the necessity of self-dependence must give each individual the right to choose his own surroundings.

The strongest reason for giving women all the opportunities for higher education, for the full development of her faculties, forces of mind and body; for giving her the most enlarged freedom of thought and action; a complete emancipation from all forms of bondage, of custom, depen-

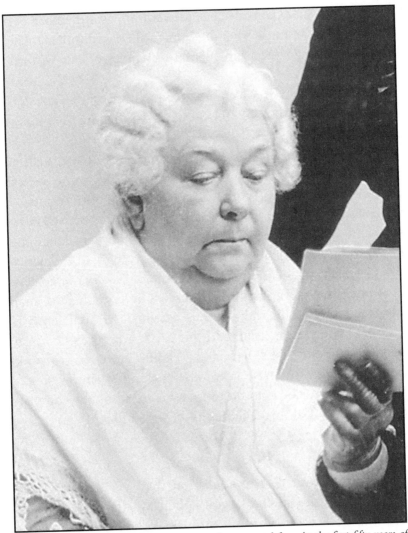

Elizabeth Cady Stanton (1815–1902) was an instrumental force in the first fifty years of the suffrage movement. The Library of Congress.

dence, superstition; from all the crippling influences of fear, is the solitude and personal responsibility of her own individual life. The strongest reason why we ask for woman a voice in the government under which she lives; in the religion she is asked to believe; equality in social life, where she is the chief factor; a place in the trades and professions, where she may earn her bread, is because of her birthright to self-sovereignty; because, as an individual, she must rely on herself. No matter how much women prefer to lean, to be protected and supported, nor how much men desire to have them do so, they must make the voyage of life alone, and for safety in an emergency they must know something of the laws of navigation. To guide our own craft, we must be captain, pilot, engineer; with chart and compass to stand at the wheel; to watch the wind and waves and know when to take in the sail, and to read the signs in the firmament over all. It matters not whether the solitary voyager is man or woman. Nature having endowed them equally, leaves them to their own skill and judgment in the hour of danger, and, if not equal to the occasion, alike they perish.

The Importance of the Individual

To appreciate the importance of fitting every human soul for independent action, think for a moment of the immeasurable solitude of self. We come into the world alone, unlike all who have gone before us; we leave it alone under circumstances peculiar to ourselves. No mortal ever has been, no mortal ever will be like the soul just launched on the sea of life. There can never again be just such a combination of prenatal influences; never again just such environments as make up the infancy, youth, and manhood of this one. Nature never repeats herself, and the possibilities of one human soul will never be found in another. No one has ever found two blades of ribbon grass alike, and no one will ever find two human beings alike. Seeing, then, what must be the infinite diversity in human character, we can in a measure appreciate the loss to a nation when any large class of the people is uneducated and unrepresented in the government. We ask for the complete development of every individual, first, for his own benefit and happiness. In fitting out an army we give each soldier his own knapsack, arms, powder, his blanket, cup, knife, fork and spoon. We provide alike for all their individual necessities, then each man bears his own burden.

Again we ask complete individual development for the general good; for the consensus of the competent on the whole round of human interests; on all questions of national life, and here each man must bear his share of the general burden. It is sad to see how soon friendless children are left to bear their own burdens before they can analyze their feelings; before they can even tell their joys and sorrows, they are thrown on their own resources. The great lesson that nature seems to teach us at all ages is self-dependence, self-protection, self-support. What a touching instance of a child's solitude; of that hunger of the heart for love and recognition, in the case of the little girl who helped to dress a Christmas tree for the children of the family in which she served. On finding there was no present for herself she slipped away in the darkness and spent the night in an open field sitting on a stone, and when found in the morning was weeping as if her heart would break. No mortal will ever know the thoughts that passed through the mind of that friendless child in the long hours of that cold night, with only the silent stars to keep her company. The mention of her case in the daily papers moved many generous hearts to send her presents, but in the hours of her keenest suffering she was thrown wholly on herself for consolation.

Situations of Solitude

In youth our most bitter disappointments, our brightest hopes and ambitions are known only to ourselves; even our friendship and love we never fully share with another; there is something of every passion in every situation we conceal. Even so in our triumphs and our defeats. The successful candidate for the Presidency and his opponent each have a solitude peculiarly his own, and good form forbids either to speak to his pleasure or regret. The solitude of the king on his throne and the prisoner in his cell differs in character and degree, but it is solitude nevertheless.

We ask no sympathy from others in the anxiety and agony of a broken friendship or shattered love. When death sunders our nearest ties, alone we sit in the shadow of our affliction. Alike mid the greatest triumphs and darkest tragedies of life we walk alone. On the divine heights of human attainments, eulogized and worshipped as a hero or saint, we stand alone. In ignorance, poverty, and vice, as a pauper or criminal, alone we starve or steal; alone we suffer the sneers and rebuffs of our fellows; alone we are hunted and hounded through dark courts and alleys, in by-ways and highways; alone we stand in the judgment seat; alone in the prison cell we lament our crimes and misfortunes; alone we expiate them on the gallows. In hours like these we realize the awful solitude of individual life, its pains, its penalties, its responsibilities: hours in which the youngest and most helpless are thrown on their own resources for guidance and consolation. Seeing then that life must ever be a march and a battle, that each soldier must be equipped for his own protection, it is the height of cruelty to rob the individual of a single natural right.

To throw obstacles in the way of a complete education is like putting out the eyes; to deny the rights of property, like cutting off the hands. To deny political equality is to rob the ostracised of all self-respect; of credit in the market place; of recompense in the world of work; of a voice in those who make and administer the law; a choice in the jury before whom they are tried, and in the judge who decides their punishment. Shakespeare's play of *Titus Andronicus* contains a terrible satire on woman's position in the nineteenth century— "Rude men" (the play tells us) "seized the king's daughter, cut out her tongue, cut off her hands, and then bade her go [call] for water and wash her hands." What a picture of woman's position. Robbed of her natural rights, handicapped by law and custom at every turn, yet compelled to fight her own battles, and in the emergencies of life to fall back on herself for protection.

Women Alone

The girl of sixteen, thrown on the world to support herself, to make her own place in society, to resist the temptations that surround her and maintain a spotless integrity, must do all this by native force or superior education. She does not acquire this power by being trained to trust others and distrust herself. If she wearies of the struggle, finding it hard work to swim upstream, and allows herself to drift with the current, she will find plenty of company, but not one to share her misery in the hour of her deepest humiliation. If she tries to retrieve her position, to conceal the past, her life is hedged about with fears lest willing hands should tear the veil from what she fain would hide. Young and friendless, she knows the bitter solitude of self.

How the little courtesies of life on the surface of society, deemed so important from man towards woman, fade into utter insignificance in view of the deeper tragedies in which she must play her part alone, where no human aid is possible.

The young wife and mother, at the head of some establishment with a kind husband to shield her from the adverse winds of life, with wealth, fortune and position, has a certain harbor of safety, secure against the ordinary ills of life. But to manage a household, have a desirable influence in society, keep her friends and the affections of her husband, train her children and servants well, she must have rare common sense, wisdom, diplomacy, and a knowledge of human nature. To do all this she needs the cardinal virtues and the strong points of character that the most successful statesman possesses.

An uneducated woman, trained to dependence, with no resources in herself must make a failure of any position in life. But society says women do not need a knowledge of the world;

the liberal training that experience in public life must give, all the advantages of collegiate education; but when for the lack of all this, the woman's happiness is wrecked, alone she bears her humiliation; and the solitude of the weak and the ignorant is indeed pitiable. In the wild chase for the prizes of life they are ground to powder.

Engaging the Mind

In age, when the pleasures of youth are passed, children grown up, married and gone, the hurry and bustle of life in a measure over, when the hands are weary of active service, when the old armchair and the fireside are the chosen resorts, then men and women alike must fall back on their own resources. If they cannot find companionship in books, if they have no interest in the vital questions of the hour, no interest in watching the consummation of reforms, with which they might have been identified, they soon pass into their dotage. The more fully the faculties of the mind are developed and kept in use, the longer the period of vigor and active interest in all around us continues. If from a lifelong participation in public affairs a woman feels responsible for the laws regulating our system of education, the discipline of our jails and prisons, the sanitary condition of our private homes, public buildings, and thoroughfares, an interest in commerce, finance, our foreign relations, in any or all these questions, her solitude will at least be respectable, and she will not be driven to gossip or scandal for entertainment.

The chief reason for opening to every soul the doors to the whole round of human duties and pleasures is the individual development thus attained, the resources thus provided under all circumstances to mitigate the solitude that at times must come to everyone. I once asked Prince Krapotkin, a Russian nihilist, how he endured his long years in prison, deprived of books, pen, ink, and paper. "Ah," he said, "I thought out many questions in which I had a deep interest. In the pursuit of an idea I took no note of time. When tired of solving knotty problems I recited all the beautiful passages in prose or verse I had ever learned. I became acquainted with myself and my own resources. I had a world of my own, a vast empire, that no Russian jailor or Czar could invade." Such is the value of liberal thought and broad culture when shut off from all human companionship, bringing comfort and sunshine within even the four walls of a prison cell.

Individuals and Strength of Character

As women ofttimes share a similar fate, should they not have all the consolation that the most liberal education can give? Their suffering in the prisons of St. Petersburg; in the long, weary marches to Siberia, and in the mines, working side by side with men, surely call for all the self-support that the most exalted sentiments of heroism can give. When suddenly roused at midnight, with the startling cry of "fire! fire!" to find the house over their heads in flames, do women wait for men to point the way to safety? And are the men, equally bewildered and half suffocated with smoke, in a position to do more than try to save themselves?

At such times the most timid women have shown a courage and heroism in saving their husbands and children that has surprised everybody. Inasmuch, then, as woman shares equally the joys and sorrows of time and eternity, is it not the height of presumption in man to propose to represent her at the ballot box and the throne of grace, to do her voting in the state, her praying in the church, and to assume the position of high priest at the family altar?

Nothing strengthens the judgment and quickens the conscience like individual responsibility. Nothing adds such dignity to character as the recognition of one's self-sovereignty; the right to an equal place, everywhere conceded; a place earned by personal merit, not an artificial attainment, by inheritance, wealth, family, and position. Seeing, then, that the responsibilities of life rest equally on man and woman, that their destiny is the same, they need the same preparation for time and eternity. The talk of sheltering woman from the fierce storms of life is the sheerest mockery, for they beat on her from every point of the compass, just as they do on man, and with more fatal results, for he has been trained to protect himself, to resist, to conquer. Such are the facts in human experience, the responsibilities of individual sovereignty. Rich and poor, intelligent and ignorant, wise and foolish, virtuous and vicious, man and woman, it is ever the same, each soul must depend wholly on itself.

Whatever the theories may be of woman's dependence on man, in the supreme moments of her life he can not bear her burdens. Alone she goes to the gates of death to give life to every man that is born into the world. No one can share her fears, no one can mitigate her pangs; and if her sorrow is greater than she can bear, alone she passes beyond the gates into the vast unknown.

From the mountain tops of Judea, long ago, a heavenly voice bade His disciples "Bear ye one another's burdens," but humanity has not yet risen to that point of self-sacrifice, and if ever so willing, how few the burdens are that one soul can bear for another. In the highways of Palestine; in prayer and fasting on the solitary mountain top; in the Garden of Gethsemane; before the judgment seat of Pilate; betrayed by one of His trusted disciples at His last supper; in His agonies on the cross, even Jesus of Nazareth, in these last sad days on earth, felt the awful solitude of self. Deserted by man, in agony he cries, "My God! My God! why hast Thou forsaken me?" And so it ever must be in the conflicting scenes of life, in the long, weary march, each one walks alone. We may have many friends, love, kindness, sympathy, and charity to smoothe our pathway in everyday life, but in the tragedies and triumphs of human experience each mortal stands alone.

Curriculum for Women and Men

But when all artificial trammels are removed, and women are recognized as individuals, responsible for their own environments, thoroughly educated for all positions in life they may be called to fill; with all the resources in themselves that liberal thought and broad culture can give; guided by their own conscience and judgment; trained to self-protection by a healthy development of the muscular system and skill in the use of weapons of defense, and stimulated to self-support by a knowledge of the business world and the pleasure that pecuniary independence must ever give; when women are trained in this way they will, in a measure, be fitted for those hours of solitude that come alike to all, whether prepared or otherwise. As in our extremity we must depend on ourselves, the dictates of wisdom point to complete individual development.

In talking of education how shallow the argument, that each class must be educated for the special work it proposes to do, and all those faculties not needed in this special walk must lie dormant and utterly wither for want of use, when, perhaps, these will be very faculties needed in life's greatest emergencies. Some say, Where is the use of drilling girls in the languages, the sciences, in law, medicine, theology? As wives, mothers, housekeepers, cooks, they need a different curriculum from boys who are to fill all positions. The chief cooks in our great hotels and ocean steamers are men. In our large cities men run the bakeries; they make our bread, cake and pies. They manage the laundries; they are now considered our best milliners and dressmakers. Because some men fill these departments of usefulness, shall we regulate the curriculum in Harvard and Yale to their present necessities? If not, why this talk in our best colleges of a curriculum for girls who are crowding into the trades and professions; teachers in all our public schools, rapidly filling many lucrative and honorable positions in life? They are showing, too, their calmness and courage in the most trying hours of human experience.

Nature Is the Greatest of Teachers

You have probably all read in the daily papers of the terrible storm in the Bay of Biscay when a tidal wave made such havoc on the shore, wrecking vessels, unroofing houses, and carrying destruction everywhere. Among other buildings the woman's prison was demolished. Those who escaped saw men struggling to reach the shore. They promptly by clasping hands made a chain of themselves and pushed out into the sea, again and again, at the risk of their lives, until they had brought six men to shore, carried them to a shelter, and did all in their power for their comfort and protection.

What special school training could have prepared these women for this sublime moment in their lives? In times like this humanity rises above all college curriculums and recognizes Nature as the greatest of all teachers in the hour of danger and death. Women are already the equals of men in the whole realm of thought, in art, science, literature, and government. With telescopic vision they explore the starry firmament and bring back the history of the planetary world. With chart and compass they pilot ships across the mighty deep, and with skillful finger send electric messages around the globe. In galleries of art the beauties of nature and the virtues of humanity are immortalized by them on canvas and by their inspired touch dull blocks of marble are transformed into angels of light.

In music they speak again the language of Mendelssohn, Beethoven, Chopin, Schumann, and are worthy interpreters of their great thoughts. The poetry and novels of the century are theirs, and they have touched the keynote of reform in religion, politics, and social life. They fill the editor's and professor's chair and plead at the bar of justice, walk the wards of the hospital, and speak from the pulpit and the platform; such is the type of womanhood that an enlightened public sentiment welcomes today, and such the triumph of the facts of life over the false theories of the past.

No Holding Back

Is it, then, consistent to hold the developed woman of this day within the same narrow political limits as the dame with the spinning wheel and knitting needle occupied in the past? No! no! Machinery has taken the labors of woman as well as man on its tireless shoulders; the loom and the spinning wheel are but dreams of the past; the pen, the brush, the easel, the chisel, have taken their places, while the hopes and ambitions of women are essentially changed.

We see reason sufficient in the outer conditions of human beings for individual liberty and development, but when we consider the self dependence of every human soul we see the need of courage, judgment, and the exercise of every faculty of mind and body, strengthened and developed by use, in woman as well as man.

Whatever may be said of man's protecting power in ordinary conditions, mid all the terrible disasters by land and sea, in the supreme moments of danger, alone woman must ever meet the horrors of the situation; the Angel of Death even makes no royal pathway for her. Man's love and sympathy enter only into the sunshine of our lives. In that solemn solitude of self, that links us with the immeasurable and the eternal, each soul lives alone forever. A recent writer says:

> I remember once, in crossing the Atlantic, to have gone upon the deck of the ship at midnight, when a dense black cloud enveloped the sky, and the great deep was roaring madly under the lashes of demoniac winds. My feeling was not of danger or fear (which is a base surrender of the immortal soul), but of utter desolation and loneliness; a little speck of life shut in by a tremendous darkness. Again I remember to have climbed the slopes of the Swiss Alps, up beyond the point where vegetation ceases, and the stunted conifers no longer struggle against the unfeeling blasts. Around me lay a huge confusion of rocks, out of which the

gigantic toe peaks shot into the measureless blue of the heavens, and again my only feeling was the awful solitude.

And yet, there is a solitude, which each and every one of us has always carried with him more inaccessible than the ice-cold mountains, more profound than the midnight sea; the solitude of self. Our inner being, which we call ourself, no eye nor touch of man or angel has ever pierced. It is more hidden than the caves of the gnome; the sacred adytum of the oracle; the hidden chamber of eleusinian mystery, for to it only omniscience is permitted to enter.

Such is individual life. Who, I ask you, can take, dare take, on himself the rights, the duties, the responsibilities of another human soul?

The "Night of Terror"

Mary A. Nolan

In 1917 Mary A. Nolan of Jacksonville, Florida, joined the National Woman's Party and volunteered to go to Washington, D.C., to demonstrate for women's right to vote. While picketing outside the White House, she and many other women were arrested on November 10, 1917, and sent to the Occoquan workhouse when they refused to post bail. In the following account, Nolan describes her terror-filled first night in the dungeons of the workhouse and the rough treatment that she and the other women received there. She was released after six days, leaving the other women behind. Nolan was seventy-three when she traveled from Florida to Washington, D.C., to picket on behalf of women's right to vote, making her the oldest suffrage prisoner.

When Mrs. Gould and Miss Younger asked Florida women to go to Washington to help, I volunteered. I am seventy-three, but except for my lame foot I was well. . . .

I picketed three times with these splendid women, carrying a purple, white and gold suffrage flag. The third time we spent the night in the House of Detention because we refused to give bail. . . .

They ran through that "trial" rapidly the next day. We did not answer them or pay any attention. We knew, of course, that we would all be convicted and sentenced for months, just as the hundred and more other women who had done this thing for suffrage. . . .

The Workhouse

It was about half past seven at night when we got to Occoquan workhouse. A woman was standing behind a desk when we were brought into this office, and there were six men also

Mary A. Nolan, *The Suffragist*, December 1, 1917.

in the room. Mrs. Lewis, who spoke for all of us, refused to talk to the woman—who, I learned, was Mrs. Herndon—and said she must speak to Mr. Whittaker, the superintendent of the place.

"You'll sit here all night then," said Mrs. Herndon. I saw men beginning to come up on the porch through the window. But I didn't think anything about it. Mrs. Herndon called my name, but I did not answer. "You had better answer or it will be the worse for you," said one man. "I'll take you and handle you, and you'll be sorry you made me," said another. The police woman who came with us begged us to answer to our names. We could see she was afraid.

Suddenly the door literally burst open and Whittaker rushed in like a tornado; some men followed him. We could see the crowds of them on the porch. They were not in uniform. They looked as much like tramps as anything. They seemed to come in—and in—and in. One had a face that made me think of an orang-outang. Mrs. Lewis stood up—we had been sitting and lying on the floor; we were so tired—but she had hardly began to speak, saying we demanded to be treated as political prisoners when Whittaker said:

"You shut up! I have men here glad to handle you. Seize her!" I just saw men spring toward her and some one screamed, "They have taken Mrs. Lewis," when a man sprang at me, and caught me by the shoulder. I am used to being careful of my bad foot and I remember saying, "I'll come with you; don't drag me; I have a lame foot." But I was jerked down the steps and away into the dark. I didn't have my feet on the ground; I guess that saved me. I heard Mrs. Cosu, who was being dragged after me, call, "Be careful of your foot."

The Dungeons

It was very black. The other building as we came to it, was low and dark. I only remember the American flag flying above because it caught the light from a window in a wing. We were rushed into a large room that we found opened on a long hall with brick dungeons on each side. "Punishment cells" is what they call them. They are dungeons. Mine was filthy; it had no window save a little slit at the top and no furniture but a sheet-iron bed and an open toilet flushed from outside the cell.

In the hall outside was a man called Captain Reems. He had on a uniform and was brandishing a stick as thick as my fist and shouting as we were shoved into the corridor. "Damn you, get in here!" I saw Dorothy Day brought in. She is a very slight girl. The two men were twisting her arms above her head. Then suddenly they lifted her up and banged her down over the arm of an iron bench—twice. As they ran me past she was lying there with her arms out, and I heard one of the men yell, "The——suffrager! My mother aint no suffrager. I'll put you through——."

Ill and Ignored

At the end of the corridor they pushed me through a door. I lost my balance and fell on the iron bed. Mrs. Cosu struck the wall. Then they threw in two mats and two dirty blankets. There was no light but from the corridor. The door was barred from top to bottom. The walls were brick cemented over. It was bitter cold. Mrs. Cosu would not let me lie on the floor. She put me on the couch and stretched out on the floor. We had only lain there a few minutes trying to get our breath when Mrs. Lewis, doubled over and handled like a sack of something, was literally thrown in by two men: Her head struck the iron bed and she fell.

We thought she was dead. She didn't move. We were crying over her as we lifted her to the bed and stretched her out, when we heard Miss Burns call: "Where is Mrs. Lewis?"

Mrs. Cosu called out, "They've just thrown her in here." We were roughly told by the guard not to dare to speak again, or we would be put in straight-jackets. We were so terrified we kept very still. Mrs. Lewis was not unconscious; she was only stunned. But Mrs. Cosu was desperately ill as the night wore on. She had a bad heart attack, and then vomiting. We called and called. We asked them to send our doctor because we thought she was dying; there was a woman guard and a man in the corridor, but they paid no attention. A cold wind blew in on us from the outside, and we all lay there shivering and only half conscious until early morning. . . .

Released After Six Days

I was released on the sixth day, and passed the dispensary as I came out. There were a group of my friends, Mrs. Brannan and Mrs. Morey and several others. They had on coarse striped dresses and big grotesque heavy shoes. I burst into tears as they led me away, my term having expired. I didn't want to desert them like that, but I had done all I could.

Congress Passes the Nineteenth Amendment

The New York Times

The following article appeared in The New York Times *on June 5, 1919, describing the U.S. Congress's passage of the Nineteenth Amendment. The amendment was approved in the Senate by a vote of 56 to 25 after passing the House of Representatives by a vote of 304 to 89. Before the vote was called, several senators had tried to block the roll call by various methods. When the vote total was announced, suffragists in the Senate galleries gave a two-minute ovation. The author describes the signing of the bill and discusses the prospects of the amendment being ratified by the individual states.* The New York Times, *founded in 1851, is one of the best-known daily newspapers in the world.*

After a long and persistent fight advocates of woman suffrage won a victory in the Senate today when that body, by a vote of 56 to 25, adopted the Susan Anthony amendment to the Constitution. The suffrage supporters had two more than the necessary two-thirds vote of Senators present. Had all the Senators known to be in favor of suffrage been present the amendment would have had 66 votes, or two more than a two-thirds vote of the entire Senate.

The amendment, having already been passed by the House, where the vote was 304 to 89, now goes to the States for ratification, where it will be passed upon in the form in which it has been adopted by Congress, as follows:

> "Article-, Section 1. The right of citizens of the United States to vote shall not be denied or abridged by the United States or by any State on account of sex."

The New York Times, "Suffrage Wins in Senate; Now Goes to States," June 5, 1919. www.nytimes.com.

"Section 2. Congress shall have power, by appropriate legislation, to enforce the provisions of this article."

Leaders of the National Woman's Party announced tonight
that they would at once embark upon a campaign to obtain
ratification of the amendment by the necessary three-fourths
of the States so that women might have the vote in the next
Presidential election [in 1920]. To achieve this ratification it
will be necessary to hold special sessions of some Legislatures
which otherwise would not convene until after the Presidential election in 1920. Miss Alice Paul, Chairman of the
Woman's Party, predicted that the campaign for ratification
would succeed and that women would vote for the next President.

Suffragists thronged the Senate galleries in anticipation of
the final vote, and when the outcome was announced by President Pro Tem. [Albert B.] Cummins they broke into deafening
applause. For two minutes the demonstration went on, Senator Cummins making no effort to check it. . . .

The vote came after four hours of debate, during which
Democratic Senators opposed to the amendment filibustered
to prevent a roll call until their absent Senators could be protected by pairs. They gave up the effort finally as futile.

Changes Defeated

Before the final vote was taken Senator [Oscar Wilder] Under-
wood of Alabama, called for a vote on his amendment to submit the suffrage amendment to Constitutional conventions of
the various States, instead of to the Legislatures, for ratification. This was defeated by a vote of 45 against to 28 in favor.

Senator [Edward J.] Gay of Louisiana offered an amendment proposing enforcement of the suffrage amendment by
the States, instead of by the Federal Government. Senator Gay
said that from a survey of the States he could predict that
thirteen States would not ratify the amendment, enough to
block it. His amendment was defeated, 62 to 19.

This poster, "Votes for Women" is a takeoff of the "Spirit of '76." Images like this one fueled passage of the Nineteenth Amendment. The Library of Congress.

During debate, Senator [James W.] Wadsworth [Jr.] of New York, who has been an uncompromising opponent of woman suffrage, explained his attitude as being actuated by the motive of preserving to the States the right to determine the question, each State for itself.

"No vote of mine cast upon this amendment would deprive any of the electors of my State of any privilege they now enjoy," said the Senator. "I feel so strongly that the people of the several States should be permitted to decide for themselves, that am frank to say that, if this amendment, instead of being drafted to extend woman suffrage all over the country, were drafted to forbid the extension of the franchise to women in the States, I would vote against it. Even though one might be opposed on general principles to the extension of the franchise to women, one cannot logically object to the people of a State settling that question for themselves.

"It seems to me that it is incumbent upon a Senator in considering his attitude on this matter to regard the nation as a whole and to give consideration to the wishes of the people of the various States which have expressed themselves from time to time."

Overriding State Votes

Senator Wadsworth spoke of the results in Massachusetts, New Jersey, Pennsylvania, West Virginia, Ohio, Louisiana, Texas, Wisconsin, and other States where woman suffrage was defeated at the polls.

"Now the question is," he resumed, "whether the people of these States are competent to settle the question for themselves. There is no tremendous emergency facing the country, no revolution or rebellion threatened, which would seem to make it necessary to impose on the people of these States a thing they have said as free citizens they do not require or desire. Is it contrary to the spirit of American institutions that they shall be left free to decide these things for themselves?

"My contention has been, with respect to an amendment to the Constitution, that, if it be placed there, it should command the reverence and devotion of all the people of the country. The discussion here yesterday makes it perfectly apparent that, in part at least, in a certain section of this country, this proposed amendment will be a dead letter. No pretense is made that it will be lived up to in spirit as well as in letter. That same attitude has been manifest in the discussion of the last amendment to the Constitution, ratified last Winter. Today there are thousands of people all over the United States who are attempting to contrive ways by which the prohibition amendment can be evaded. This attitude shows an utter lack of appreciation of the Constitution as a sacred instrument, a lack of realization of the spirit of self-government."

Senator [Elison D.] Smith of South Carolina opposed giving women the right to vote, he said, because to allow it would induce "sectional anarchy."

Signing of the Resolution

Immediately after its passage by the Senate the Suffrage Amendment was signed. In appreciation of the fifty-year campaign of the National American Woman Suffrage Association, the guests were limited to representatives of that association and members of Congress, and the gold pen used was presented to the national association. The women chosen to represent the national association were Mrs. Wood Park of Massachusetts, who for two years has been in charge of the association's Congressional work: Mrs. Helen Gardener of Washington, D.C.; Mrs. Ida Husted Harper of New York, Mrs. Harriet Taylor Upton of Ohio, Miss Mary G. Hay, and Miss Marjorie Shuler of New York.

Besides Speaker [of the House Frederick H.] Gillett, who signed the bill, the members of the House present were Frank W. Mondell, majority leader; Champ Clark, minority leader and ex-Speaker, under whom the amendment first passed the House, and John E. Raker, Chairman of the committee which won the suffrage victory in the House last year.

The Senators present at the signing of the bill for the Senate were Albert B. Cummins, President Pro Tempore, who signed the measure; James E. Watson, Chairman of the Suffrage Committee; Charles Curtis, Republican whip; A.A. Jones, Chairman of the Suffrage Committee in the last Congress; Thomas J. Walsh of Montana, Morris Sheppard, Joseph E. Ransdell, and Reed Smoot.

To celebrate the passage of the amendment the national association will give a reception next Tuesday evening at its Washington headquarters to the members of the House and Senate who voted for the resolution and to their wives. These will be the only guests.

Miss Paul, Chairman of the National Woman's Party, issued a statement, in which she said: "There is no doubt of ratification by the States. We enter upon the campaign for special sessions of Legislatures to accomplish this ratification before 1920 in the full assurance that we shall win."

"The last stage of the fight is to obtain ratification of the amendment so women may vote in the Presidential election in 1920," said Mrs. Carrie Chapman Catt, President of the association. "This we are confident will be achieved. The friends of woman suffrage in both parties have carried out their word. In the result we can turn our backs upon the end of a long and arduous struggle, needlessly darkened and embittered by the stubbornness of a few at the expense of the many. 'Eyes front,' is the watchword as we turn upon the struggle for ratification by the States."

Prospects of Ratification

Suffrage leaders say quick ratification is assured in twenty-eight States in which women now have full or Presidential suffrage. These States are Wyoming, Colorado, Utah, Idaho, Washington, California, Kansas, Arizona, Oregon, Montana, New York, Oklahoma, South Dakota, Michigan, Illinois, Nebraska,

Rhode Island, North Dakota, Iowa, Wisconsin, Indiana, Maine, Minnesota, Missouri, Tennessee, Arkansas, Nevada, and Texas.

Legislatures now in session are: Illinois, will adjourn late in June; Pennsylvania, Massachusetts, adjourn end of June or first of July; Wisconsin, Florida, in session until June 1, cannot ratify, because an election must intervene between submission of amendment and ratification.

Legislatures to meet comparatively soon, or with prospects of meeting soon, are: Michigan and Texas, extra sessions called in June; Georgia, to meet this month; Alabama, to meet in July; Louisiana, possibility of extra session before September; New Jersey, movement for extra session soon; Maine, special session in October; Iowa, special session in January; Kentucky, South Carolina, and Mississippi, meet in January; Virginia, meets in February; Maryland, meets during 1920; Ohio, meets in June.

History of Suffrage

Today's victory for suffrage ends a fight that really dates from the American Revolution. Women voted under several of the Colonial Governments. During the Revolution women demanded to be included in the Government. Abigail Adams wrote her husband, John Adams, "If women are not represented in this new republic there will be another revolution." From the time of the Revolution women agitated for suffrage by means of meetings and petitions. In 1848 a woman's rights convention was held at Seneca Falls, N.Y., arranged by Lucretia Mott and Elizabeth Cady Stanton as the first big suffrage demonstration. From 1848 to the civil war efforts were made to have State laws altered to include women, and Susan B. Anthony became leader of the movement.

For five years after the civil war suffragists tried to secure interpretation of the Fourteenth and Fifteenth Amendments which would permit them to vote. In 1872 Miss Anthony made a test vote at the polls, was arrested, and refused to pay her fine, but was never jailed. In 1875 Miss Anthony drafted the proposed Federal amendment, the same one that was voted on today. In 1878 the amendment was introduced in the Senate by Senator [A.A.] Sargent of California. It has been voted on in the Senate five times, including today. In 1878 the vote was 16 yeas to 34 nays; in 1914 it failed by 11 votes, in 1918 it failed by two votes, and on Feb. 10, 1919, it failed by one vote. It has been voted on three times in the House. It failed there in 1915 by 78 votes. In 1918 it passed the House with one vote to spare. On May 21, 1919, it passed the House with 14 votes more than the necessary two-thirds.

Foreign countries or divisions of countries in which women have suffrage are: Isle of Man, granted 1881; New Zealand, 1893; Australia, 1902; Finland, 1906; Norway, 1907; Iceland, 1913; Denmark, 1915; Russia, 1917; Canada, Austria, England, Germany, Hungary, Ireland, Poland, Scotland, and Wales, 1918; Holland and Sweden, 1919.

Women Finally Get the Vote

Associated Press

The following Associated Press article addresses the adoption of the Nineteenth Amendment to the U.S. Constitution, which was formally enacted on August 26, 1920, by Secretary of State Bainbridge Colby. His remarks regarding the historic occasion are included, and the author describes the quiet circumstances surrounding the signing. Formed in 1846, the Associated Press is an American cooperative news agency owned by its contributing newspapers and news stations.

Without pomp or ceremony, Secretary [of State Bainbridge] Colby today signed the proclamation declaring the woman suffrage amendment "to all intents and purposes a part of the Constitution of the United States."

The Secretary's signature was affixed to the proclamation at his home at 8 a.m. a few hours after he had received from Gov. [Albert H.] Roberts the certificate that final favorable action on the amendment has been taken by the Tennessee Legislature.

The quiet manner in which Colby acted was a disappointment to some suffrage workers who had hoped to make a ceremony of his act, but they contented themselves with their own jubilation ceremonies, including a mass meeting tonight. They united in statements that nothing now can be done to prevent the women from voting in November.

"The seal of the United States has been duly affixed to the certificate and the suffrage amendment is now the Nineteenth Amendment to the Constitution," Secretary Colby announced on reaching his office.

Associated Press, "Women Get the Vote," August 26, 1920.

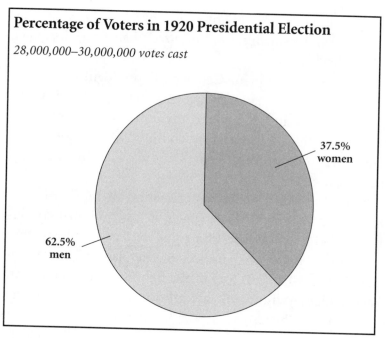

Percentage of Voters in 1920 Presidential Election

28,000,000–30,000,000 votes cast

37.5% women

62.5% men

A Simple Duty

A desire to avoid the limelight and to prevent arousing the feeling among suffrage workers as to whom should be present prompted the quiet setting. Colby explained, also, that his only purpose was to pursue a simple duty.

Colby was awakened at 3:45 a.m. by a State Department employee, who notified him that the Tennessee certification had arrived. The Secretary then called for F.K. Neilsen, department solicitor, to examine the Tennessee papers, also instructing the solicitor to bring the proclamation to the Secretary's home at 8 o'clock.

After the visit of her delegation to the State Department, Miss Alice Paul left here for New York to call a meeting of the Executive Committee of the National Woman's party to fix a date for a party convention of future work. Other leaders of the Woman's party, including Mrs. Abby Scott Baker, the party's political chairman, discussed with Solicitor-General [William L.] Frierson and other officials any possible legal steps the anti-suffragists might take. They later said they believed that "all reasonable fear" of attack had been dissipated by Mr. Colby's action.

Mrs. [Carrie Chapman] Catt who is president of the National American Woman Suffrage Association, called at the White House late in the day and presented to President Wilson a book entitled "Tribute to Woodrow Wilson," containing testimonials from suffrage leaders and associations in every State.

The preface contained an appreciation of the President's effort to bring about suffrage, which, it was said, had continued since 1916. The celebration tonight at a downtown theater was given under the auspices of the National League of Women Voters. Mrs. Catt told of the fight for the amendment, while President Wilson sent his greetings to the new voters and Secretary Colby also addressed the meeting.

Secretary Colby's Statement of Congratulations

Secretary Colby's statement follows.

"The certified record of the action of the Legislature of the State of Tennessee on the suffrage amendment was received by mail this morning. Immediately on its receipt the record was brought to my house. This was in compliance with my directions and in accordance with numerous requests for prompt action.

"I thereupon signed the certificate required of the Secretary of State this morning at 8 o'clock in the presence of Mr. F.K. Nielsen, the solicitor of the State Department, and Mr. Charles L. Cook, also of the State Department. The seal of the United States has been duly affixed to the certificate and the suffrage amendment is now the Nineteenth Amendment of the Constitution.

"It was decided not to accompany the simple ministerial action on my part with any ceremony or setting. This secondary aspect of the subject has, regretfully, been the source of considerable contention as to who shall participate in it and who shall not.

"Inasmuch as I am not interested in the aftermath of any of the frictions or collisions which may have been developed in the long struggle for the ratification of the amendment, I contented myself with the performance in the simplest manner of the duties devolved upon me under the law.

"I congratulate the women of the country upon the successful culmination of their efforts which have been sustained in the face of many discouragements, and which have now conducted them to the achievement of that great object.

"The day marks the opening of a great and new era in the political life of the nation. I confidently believe that every salutary, forward and upward force in our public life will receive fresh vigor and reinforcement from the enfranchisement of the women of the country.

"To the leaders of this great movement I tender my sincere congratulations. To everyone, from the President, who uttered the call to duty, whenever the cause seemed to falter, to the humblest worker in this great reform, the praise not only of this generation, but of posterity, will be freely given."

The proclamation recounts the process by which the new Article XIX, of the Constitution, was presented and ratified, naming the ratifying States, and continues:

"Now, therefore, be it known that I, Bainbridge Colby, Secretary of State of the United States, by virtue and in pursuance of Section 205, of the revised statutes of the United States, do hereby certify that the amendment aforesaid has become valid to all intents and purposes as a part of the Constitution of the United States."

The Amendment Proclamation

Following is the proclamation signed by Secretary Colby:

To all to whom these presents shall come, greeting:

Know we, that the Congress of the United States at the first session Sixty-sixth Congress begun at Washington on the 19th day of May in the year one thousand nine hundred and nineteen, passed a resolution as follows: to wit—.

Proposing an amendment to the Constitution extending the right of suffrage to women.

Resolved by the Senate and House of Representatives of the United States of America in Congress assembled (two-thirds of each House concurring therein) that the following article is proposed as an amendment to the Constitution which shall be valid to all intents and purposes as part of the Constitution when ratified by the Legislature of three-fourths of the several States.

The right of citizens of the United States to vote shall not be denied or abridged by the United States or by any State on account of sex.

Congress shall have power to enforce this article by appropriate legislation.

And, further, that it appears from official documents on file in the Department of State that the amendment to the Constitution of the United States proposed as aforesaid has been ratified by the legislators of the States of Arizona, Arkansas, California, Colorado, Idaho, Illinois, Indiana, Iowa, Kansas, Kentucky, Maine, Massachusetts, Michigan, Minnesota. Missouri, Montana, Nebraska, Nevada. New Hampshire, New Jersey, New Mexico, North Dakota, New York, Ohio, Oklahoma, Oregon, Pennsylvania, Rhode Island, South Dakota, Tennessee, Texas, Utah, Washington, West Virginia, Wisconsin and Wyoming.

And, further, that the States whose Legislatures have so ratified the said proposed amendment constitute three-fourths of the whole number of States in the United States.

Now, therefore, be it known that I, Bainbridge Colby, Secretary of State of the United States, by virtue and in pursuance of Section 205 of the Revised Statutes of the United

States, do hereby certify that the amendment aforesaid has become valid to all intents and purposes as a part of the Constitution of the United States.

In testimony whereof, I have hereunto set my hand and caused the seal of the Department of State to be affixed.

Done at the city of Washington, this twenty-sixth day of August, in the year of our Lord one thousand nine hundred and twenty.

[Signed.]

Bainbridge Colby

Appreciation for Senator James Phelan

Much credit for ratification of the woman suffrage amendment by the Tennessee Legislature is given Senator James D. Phelan of California, a suffragist leader here. Miss Paul, in a letter today to Senator Phelan, said:

"I take this opportunity to express to you on behalf of the National Woman's Party, representing women in every State, our appreciation of your generous and practical help in the campaign.

"Your contribution of $1000 toward the Tennessee work was of great aid in bringing about victory in making possible a more effective campaign than would otherwise have been possible.

"We deeply appreciate the continued service which you have given to the suffrage cause throughout the ratification period."

"There is absolutely nothing that can be done now to upset or nullify the ratification of suffrage by the 'Tennessee Legislature,' declared Mrs. Harriet Taylor Upton, vice-chairman of the Republican National Executive Committee and president of the Ohio Suffrage Association.

"I regard the suffrage victory in Tennessee as perfectly safe right now, and nothing can undo it. Otherwise Mrs. Catt and I never would have left Nashville and come to Washington."

Voting Rights Trials

The Trial of Susan B. Anthony

Doug Linder

In the following essay, legal historian Doug Linder discusses the circumstances surrounding the arrest and trial of Susan B. Anthony for casting her vote in a November 5, 1872, election. Anthony and her three sisters registered to vote in Rochester, New York, against the protest of election inspectors; Anthony then proceeded to cast her ballot in the election. After a complaint of illegal voting was filed against Anthony, she was detained and charged. Linder describes how Anthony took full advantage of her arrest to rally others to the cause of women's suffrage. In the end, the judge presiding over the trial, which took place in June 1873, pronounced Anthony guilty of voting illegally, without any input from the jury. Linder is a professor at the University of Missouri–Kansas City School of Law. He has written many articles about historic trials and hosts a Web site dedicated to the subject.

More than any other woman of her generation, Susan B. Anthony saw that all of the legal disabilities faced by American women owed their existence to the simple fact that women lacked the vote. When Anthony, at age 32, attended her first woman's rights convention in Syracuse in 1852, she declared "that the right which woman needed above every other, the one indeed which would secure to her all the others, was the right of suffrage." Anthony spent the next fifty-plus years of her life fighting for the right to vote. She would work tirelessly: giving speeches, petitioning Congress and state legislatures, publishing a feminist newspaper—all for a cause that would not succeed until the ratification of the Nineteenth Amendment fourteen years after her death in 1906.

Doug Linder, "The Trial of Susan B. Anthony for Illegal Voting," www.law.umkc.edu, 2001. Reproduced by permission. www.law.umkc.edu/faculty/projects/ftrials/anthony/sbaaccount.html.

Susan B. Anthony (1820–1906) was arrested for registering and then casting her ballot in an 1872 election. The Library of Congress.

She would, however, once have the satisfaction of seeing her completed ballot drop through the opening of a ballot box. It happened in Rochester, New York on November 5, 1872, and the event—and the trial for illegal voting that followed—would create an opportunity for Anthony to spread her arguments for women suffrage to a wider audience than ever before.

Registering to Vote

Anthony had been planning to vote long before 1872. She would later state that "I have been resolved for three years to vote at the first election when I had been home for thirty days before." (New York law required legal voters to reside for the thirty days prior to the election in the district where they offered their vote.) Anthony had taken the position—and argued it wherever she could—that the recently adopted Fourteenth Amendment gave women the constitutional right to vote in federal elections. The Amendment said that "all persons born and naturalized in the United States . . . are citizens of the United States," and as citizens were entitled to the "privileges" of citizens of the United States. To Anthony's way of thinking, those privileges certainly included the right to vote.

On November 1, 1872, Anthony and her three sisters entered a voter registration office set up in a barbershop. The four Anthony women were part of a group of fifty women Anthony had organized to register in her home town of Rochester. As they entered the barbershop, the women saw stationed in the office three young men serving as registrars. Anthony walked directly to the election inspectors and, as one of the inspectors would later testify, "demanded that we register them as voters."

The election inspectors refused Anthony's request, but she persisted, quoting the Fourteenth Amendment's citizenship provision and the article from the New York Constitution pertaining to voting, which contained no sex qualification. The registers remained unmoved. Finally, according to one published account, Anthony gave the men an argument that she thought might catch their attention:

"If you refuse us our rights as citizens, I will bring charges against you in Criminal Court and I will sue each of you personally for large, exemplary damages!" She added, "I know I can win. I have Judge [Henry R.] Selden as a lawyer. There is any amount of money to back me, and if I have to, I will push to the 'last ditch' in both courts."

The stunned inspectors discussed the situation. They sought the advice of the Supervisor of elections, Daniel Warner, who, according to thirty-three-year-old election inspector E.T. Marsh, suggested that they allow the women to take the oath of registry. "Young men," Marsh quoted Warner as saying, "do you know the penalty of law if you refuse to register these names?" Registering the women, the registrars were advised, "would put the entire onus of the affair on them." Following Warner's advice, the three inspectors voted to allow Anthony and her three sisters [to register] to vote in Rochester's eighth ward. Testifying later about the registration process, Anthony remembered "it was a full hour" of debate "between the supervisors, the inspectors, and myself." In all, fourteen Rochester women successfully registered that day, leading to calls in one city paper for the arrest of the voting inspectors who complied with the women's demand. The *Rochester Union and Advertiser* editorialized in its November 4 edition: "Citizenship no more carries the right to vote than it carries the power to fly to the moon . . . If these women in the Eighth Ward offer to vote, they should be challenged, and if they take the oaths and the Inspectors receive and deposit their ballots, they should all be prosecuted to the full extent of the law."

Casting Ballots

Soon after the polls opened at the West End News Depot on Election Day, November 5, Anthony and seven or eight other women cast their ballots. Inspectors voted two to one to accept Anthony's vote, and her folded ballot was deposited in a ballot box by one of the inspectors. Inspector E. T. Marsh testified later as to feeling caught between a rock and a hard place: "Decide which way we might, we were liable to prosecution. We were expected . . . to make an infallible decision, inside of two days, of a question in which some of the best minds of the country are divided." Seven or eight more women of Rochester successfully voted in the afternoon. Anthony's vote went to U. S. Grant and other Republicans, based on that party's promise to give the demands of women a respectful hearing. . . .

Arrest and Indictment

The votes of Susan Anthony and other Rochester women was a major topic of Conversation in the days that followed. . . .

A Rochester salt manufacturer and Democratic poll watcher named Sylvester Lewis filed a complaint charging Anthony with casting an illegal vote. Lewis had challenged both Anthony's registration and her subsequent vote. United States Commissioner William C. Storrs acted upon Lewis's complaint by issuing a warrant for Anthony's arrest on November 14. The warrant charged Anthony with voting in a federal election "without having a lawful right to vote and in violation of section 19 of an act of Congress" enacted in 1870, commonly called The Enforcement Act. The Enforcement Act carried a maximum penalty of $500 or three years imprisonment.

The actual arrest of Anthony was delayed for four days to allow time for Storrs to discuss the possible prosecution with the U.S. Attorney for the Northern District of New York. On November 18, a United States deputy marshal showed up at the Anthony home on Madison Street in Rochester, where he was greeted by one of Susan's sisters. At the request of the deputy, Anthony's sister summoned Susan to the parlor. Susan Anthony had been expecting her visitor. As Anthony would later tell audiences, she had previously received word from Commissioner Storrs "to call at his office." Anthony's response was characteristically plainspoken: "I sent word to him that I had no social acquaintance with him and didn't wish to call on him." . . .

Anthony was escorted to the office of Commissioner Storrs, described by Anthony as "the same dingy little room where, in the olden days, fugitive slaves were examined and returned to their masters." Upon arriving, Anthony was surprised to learn that among those arrested for their activities on November 5 were not only the fourteen other women voters, but also the ballot inspectors who had authorized their votes.

Anthony's lawyers refused to enter a plea at the time of her arrest, and Storrs scheduled a preliminary examination for November 29. At the hearing on the 29th, complainant Sylvestor Lewis and Eighth Ward Inspectors appeared as the chief witnesses against Anthony. Anthony was questioned at the hearing by one of her lawyers, John Van Voorhis. Van Voorhis tried to establish through his questions that Anthony believed that she had a legal right to vote and therefore had not violated the 1870 Enforcement Act, which prohibited only willful and knowing illegal votes. Anthony testified that she had sought legal advice from Judge Henry R. Selden prior to casting her vote, but that Selden said "he had not studied the question." Van Voorhis asked: "Did you have any doubt yourself of your right to vote?" Anthony replied, "Not a particle." Storrs adjourned the case to December 23.

Violating the Law

After listening to legal arguments in December, Commissioner Storrs concluded that Anthony probably violated the law. When Anthony—alone among those charged with Election Day offenses—refused bail, Storrs ordered her held in the custody of a deputy marshal until the grand jury had a chance to meet in January and consider issuing an indictment. Anthony saw the commissioner's decision as a ticket to Supreme Court review, and began making plans with her lawyers to file a petition for a writ of habeas corpus. In a December 26 letter, Anthony wrote confidently, "We shall be rescued from the

Marshall hands on a Writ of Habeas Corpus—& case carried to the Supreme Court of the U. S.—the speediest process of getting there." Already letters were coming in with contributions to her "Defense Fund." She was anxious to put the money to use.

By early January, Anthony was already trying to make political hay out of her arrest. She sent off "hundreds of papers" concerning her arrest to suffragist friends and politicians. She still, however, found her situation difficult to comprehend: "I never dreamed of the U.S. officers prosecuting me for voting—thought only that if I was refused I should bring action against the inspectors—But 'Uncle Sam' waxes wroth with holy indignation at such violation of his laws!!"

Anthony's attorney, Henry Selden, asked a U.S. District Judge in Albany, Nathan Hall, to issue a writ of habeas corpus ordering the release of Anthony from the marshal's custody. Hall denied Selden's request and said he would "allow defendant to go to the Supreme Court of the United States." The judge then raised Anthony's bail from $500 to $1000. Anthony again refused to pay. Selden, however, decided to pay Anthony's bail with money from his own bank account. In the courtroom hallway following the hearing, Anthony's other lawyer, John Van Voorhis, told Anthony that Selden's decision to pay her bail meant "you've lost your chance to get your case before the Supreme Court." Shaken by the news, Anthony confronted her lawyer, demanding that he explain why he paid her bail. "I could not see a lady I respected put in jail," Selden answered.

A disappointed Anthony still had a trial to face. On January 24, 1873, a grand jury of twenty men returned an indictment against Anthony charging her with "knowingly, wrongfully, and unlawfully" voting for a member of Congress "without having a lawful right to vote, . . . the said Susan B. Anthony being then and there a person of the female sex." The trial was set for May.

On the Stump

Anthony saw the four months until her trial as an opportunity to educate the citizens of Rochester and surrounding counties on the issue of women suffrage. She took to the stump, speaking in town after town on the topic, "Is it a Crime for a Citizen of the United States to Vote?"

By mid-May, Anthony's exhausting lecture tour had taken her to every one of the twenty-nine post-office districts in Monroe County. To many in her audience, Anthony was the picture of "sophisticated refinement and sincerity." The fifty-two-year-old suffragist delivered her earnest speeches dressed in a gray silk dress a white lace collar. Her smoothed hair was twisted neatly into a tight knot. She would look at her audience, ranging from a few dozen to over a hundred persons, and begin:

> Friends and Fellow-citizens: I stand before you tonight, under indictment for the alleged crime of having voted at the last Presidential election, without having a lawful right to vote. It shall be my work this evening to prove to you that in thus voting, I not only committed no crime, but, instead, simply exercised my citizen's right, guaranteed to me and all United States citizens by the National Constitution, beyond the power of any State to deny.

In her address, Anthony quoted the Declaration of Independence, the U.S. Constitution, the New York Constitution, James Madison, Thomas Paine, the Supreme Court, and several of the leading Radical Republican senators of the day to support her contention that women had a legal right as citizens to vote. She argued that natural law, as well as a proper interpretation of the Civil War Amendments, gave women the power to vote, as in this passage suggesting that women, having been in a state of servitude, were enfranchised by the recently enacted Fifteenth Amendment [1870] extending the vote to ex-slaves:

And yet one more authority; that of Thomas Paine, than whom not one of the Revolutionary patriots more ably vindicated the principles upon which our government is founded:

"The right of voting for representatives is the primary right by which other rights are protected. To take away this right is to reduce man to a state of slavery; for slavery consists in being subject to the will of another; and he that has not a vote in the election of representatives is in this case. . . ."

Is anything further needed to prove woman's condition of servitude sufficiently orthodox to entitle her to the guaranties of the fifteenth amendment? Is there a man who will not agree with me, that to talk of freedom without the ballot, is mockery—is slavery—to the women of this Republic, precisely as New England's orator Wendell Phillips, at the close of the late war, declared it to be to the newly emancipated black men?

Anthony ended her hour-long lectures by frankly attempting to influence potential jurors to vindicate her in her upcoming trial. . . .

Worries of the Prosecution

Anthony's lecture tour plainly worried her prosecutor, U.S. Attorney Richard Crowley. In a letter to Senator Benjamin F. Butler, Anthony wrote, "I have just closed a canvass of this county—from which my jurors are to be drawn—and I rather guess the U.S. District Attorney—who is very bitter—will hardly find twelve men so ignorant on the citizen's rights—as to agree on a verdict of Guilty." In May, however, Crowley convinced Judge Ward Hunt (the recently appointed justice of the U.S. Supreme Court who would hear Anthony's case) that Anthony had prejudiced potential jurors, and Hunt agreed to move the trial out of Monroe County to Canandaigua in Ontario County. Hunt set a new opening date for the trial of June 17.

Anthony responded to the judge's move by immediately launching a lecture tour in Ontario County. Anthony spoke for twenty-one days in a row, finally concluding her tour in Canandaigua, the county seat, on the night before the opening of her trial.

The Trial Begins

Going into the June trial, Anthony and her lawyers were somewhat less optimistic about the outcome than they had been a few months before. In April, the U.S. Supreme Court handed down its first two major interpretations of the recently enacted Civil War Amendments [the Thirteenth, Fourteenth, and Fifteenth amendments], rejected the claimed violations in both cases and construing key provisions narrowly. Of special concern to Anthony was the Court's decision in *Bradwell v. Illinois*, where the Court had narrowly interpreted the Fourteenth Amendment's equal protection clause to uphold a state law that prohibited women from becoming lawyers. In an April 27 letter, Anthony anxiously sought out Benjamin Butler's views of the decision, noting that "The whole Democratic press is jubilant over this infamous interpretation of the amendments."

Even without the Supreme Court's narrow interpretation of the amendments, many observers expressed skepticism about the strength of Anthony's case. An editorial in the *New York Times* concluded:

> "Miss Anthony is not in the remotest degree likely to gain her case, nor if it were ever so desirable that women should vote, would hers be a good case. When so important a change in our Constitution as she proposes is made, it will be done openly and unmistakably, and not left to the subtle interpretation of a clause adopted for a wholly different purpose.". . .

On June 17, 1873, Anthony, wearing a new bonnet faced with blue silk and draped with a veil, walked up the steps of the Canandaigua courthouse on the opening day of her trial. The second-floor courtroom was filled to capacity. The spectators included a former president, Millard Fillmore, who had traveled over from Buffalo, where he practiced law. Judge Ward Hunt sat behind the bench, looking stolid in his black broadcloth and neck wound in a white neckcloth. Anthony described Hunt as "a small-brained, pale-faced, prim-looking man, enveloped in a faultless black suit and a snowy white tie."

Richard Crowley made the opening statement for the prosecution:

We think, on the part of the Government, that there is no question about it either one way or the other, neither a question of fact, nor a question of law, and that whatever Miss Anthony's intentions may have been—whether they were good or otherwise—she did not have a right to vote upon that question, and if she did vote without having a lawful right to vote, then there is no question but what she is guilty of violating a law of the United States in that behalf enacted by the Congress of the United States.

The Defense's Argument

The prosecution's chief witness was Beverly W. Jones, a twenty-five-year-old inspector of elections. Jones testified that he witnessed Anthony cast a ballot on November 5 in Rochester's Eighth Ward. Jones added he accepted Anthony's completed ballot and placed it a ballot box. On cross-examination, Selden asked Jones if he had also been present when Anthony registered four days earlier, and whether objections to Anthony's registration had not been considered and rejected at that time. Jones agreed that was the case, and that Anthony's name had been added to the voting rolls.

The main factual argument that the defense hoped to present was that Anthony reasonably believed that she was entitled to vote, and therefore could not be guilty of the crime of "knowingly" casting an illegal vote. To support this argument, Henry Selden called himself as a witness to testify:

> Before the last election, Miss Anthony called upon me for advice, upon the question whether she was or was not a legal voter. I examined the question, and gave her my opinion, unhesitatingly, that the laws and Constitution of the United States, authorized her to vote, as well as they authorize any man to vote.

Selden then called Anthony as a witness, so she might testify as to her vote and her state of mind on Election Day. District Attorney Crowley objected: "She is not competent as a witness on her own behalf." Judge Hunt sustained the objection, barring Anthony from taking the stand. The defense rested.

The Prosecution's Case

The prosecution called to the stand John Pound, an Assistant United States Attorney who had attended a January examination in which Anthony testified about her registration and vote. Pound testified that Anthony testified at that time that she did not consult Selden until after registering to vote. Selden, after conferring with Anthony, agreed that their meeting took place immediately after her registration, rather than before as his own testimony had suggested. On cross-examination, Pound admitted that Anthony had testified at her examination that she had "not a particle" of doubt about her right as a citizen to vote. With Pound's dismissal from the stand, the evidence closed and the legal arguments began.

Closing Arguments

Selden opened his three-hour-long argument for Anthony by stressing that she was prosecuted purely on account of her gender:

> If the same act had been done by her brother under the same circumstances, the act would have been not only inno-

cent, but honorable and laudable; but having been done by a woman it is said to be a crime. The crime therefore consists not in the act done, but in the simple fact that the person doing it was a woman and not a man, I believe this is the first instance in which a woman has been arraigned in a criminal court, merely on account of her sex. . . .

Selden stressed that the vote was essential to women receiving fair treatment from legislatures: "Much has been done, but much more remains to be done by women. If they had possessed the elective franchise, the reforms which have cost them a quarter of a century of labor would have been accomplished in a year."

Central to Selden's argument that Anthony cast a legal vote was the recently enacted Fourteenth Amendment. . . .

Finally, Selden insisted that even if the Fourteenth Amendment did not make Anthony's vote legal, she could not be prosecuted because she acted in the good faith belief that her vote *was* legal. . . .

After District Attorney Crowley offered his two-hour response for the prosecution, Judge Hunt drew from his pocket a paper and began reading an opinion that he had apparently prepared before the trial started. Hunt declared, "The Fourteenth Amendment gives no right to a woman to vote, and the voting by Miss Anthony was in violation of the law." The judge rejected Anthony's argument that her good faith precluded a finding that she "knowingly" cast an illegal vote: "Assuming that Miss Anthony believed she had a right to vote, that fact constitutes no defense if in truth she had not the right. She voluntarily gave a vote which was illegal, and thus is subject to the penalty of the law." Hunt [then] surprised Anthony and her attorney by directing a verdict of guilty: "Upon this evidence I suppose there is no question for the jury and that the jury should be directed to find a verdict of guilty."

In her diary that night Anthony would angrily describe the trial as "the greatest judicial outrage history has ever recorded! We were convicted before we had a hearing and the trial was a mere farce." During the entire trial, as Henry Selden pointed out, "No juror spoke a word during the trial, from the time they were impaneled to the time they were discharged." Had the jurors had an opportunity to speak, there is reason to believe that Anthony would not have been convicted. A newspaper quoted one juror as saying, "Could I have spoken, I should have answered 'not guilty,' and the men in the jury box would have sustained me."

Sentencing

The next day Selden argued for a new trial on the ground that Anthony's constitutional right to a trial by jury had been violated. Judge Hunt promptly denied the motion. Then, before sentencing, Hunt asked, "Has the prisoner anything to say why sentence shall not be pronounced?" The exchange that followed stunned the crowd in the Canandaigua courthouse:

"Yes, your honor, I have many things to say; for in your ordered verdict of guilty, you have trampled under foot every vital principle of our government. My natural rights, my civil rights, my political rights, my judicial rights, are all alike ignored. Robbed of the fundamental privilege of citizenship, I am degraded from the status of a citizen to that of a subject; and not only myself individually, but all of my sex, are, by your honor's verdict, doomed to political subjection under this, so-called, form of government."

Judge Hunt interrupted, "The Court cannot listen to a rehearsal of arguments the prisoner's counsel has already consumed three hours in presenting."

But Anthony would not be deterred. She continued, "May it please your honor, I am not arguing the question, but simply stating the reasons why sentence cannot, in justice, be pronounced against me. Your denial of my citizen's right to vote, is the denial of my right of consent as one of the governed, the denial of my right of representation as one of the taxed, the denial of my right to a trial by a jury of my peers as an offender against law, therefore, the denial of my sacred rights to life, liberty, property and—"

"The Court cannot allow the prisoner to go on."

"But your honor will not deny me this one and only poor privilege of protest against this high-handed outrage upon my citizen's rights. May it please the Court to remember that since the day of my arrest last November, this is the first time that either myself or any person of my disfranchised class has been allowed a word of defense before judge or jury—"

"The prisoner must sit down—the Court cannot allow it."

"All of my prosecutors, from the eighth ward corner grocery politician, who entered the complaint, to the United States Marshal, Commissioner, District Attorney, District Judge, your honor on the bench, not one is my peer, but each and all are my political sovereigns; and had your honor submitted my case to the jury, as was clearly your duty, even then I should have had just cause of protest, for not one of those men was my peer; but, native or foreign born, white or black, rich or poor, educated or ignorant, awake or asleep, sober or drunk, each and every man of them was my political superior; hence, in no sense, my peer. Even, under such circumstances, a commoner of England, tried before a jury of Lords, would have far less cause to complain than should I, a woman, tried before a jury of men. Even my counsel, the Hon. Henry R. Selden, who has argued my cause so ably, so earnestly, so unanswerably before your honor, is my political sovereign. Precisely as no disfranchised person is entitled to sit upon a jury, and no woman is entitled to the franchise, so, none but a regularly admitted lawyer is allowed to practice in the courts, and no woman can gain admission to the bar—hence, jury, judge, counsel, must all be of the superior class."

"The Court must insist—the prisoner has been tried according to the established forms of law."

"Yes, your honor, but by forms of law all made by men, interpreted by men, administered by men, in favor of men, and against women; and hence, your honor's ordered verdict of guilty; against a United States citizen for the exercise of 'that citizen's right to vote,' simply because that citizen was a woman and not a man. But, yesterday, the same man made forms of law, declared it a crime punishable with $1,000 fine and six months imprisonment, for you, or me . . . to give a cup of cold water, a crust of bread, or a night's shelter to a panting fugitive as he was tracking his way to Canada. And every man or woman in whose veins coursed a drop of human sympathy violated that wicked law, reckless of consequences, and was justified in so doing. As then, the slaves who got their freedom must take it over, or under, or through the unjust forms of law, precisely so, now, must women, to get their right to a voice in this government, take it; and I have taken mine, and mean to take it at every possible opportunity."

"The Court orders the prisoner to sit down. It will not allow another word."

"When I was brought before your honor for trial, I hoped for a broad and liberal interpretation of the Constitution and its recent amendments, that should declare. . .equality of rights the national guarantee to all persons born or naturalized in the United States. But failing to get this justice—failing, even, to get a trial by a jury not of my peers—I ask not leniency at your hands—but rather the full rigors of the law—"

"The Court must insist—"

Finally, Anthony sat down, only to be immediately ordered by Judge Hunt to rise again. Hunt pronounced sentence: "The sentence of the Court is that you pay a fine of one hundred dollars and the costs of the prosecution."

Anthony protested. "May it please your honor, I shall never pay a dollar of your unjust penalty. All the stock in trade I possess is a $10,000 debt, incurred by publishing my paper—

The Revolution—four years ago, the sole object of which was to educate all women to do precisely as I have done, rebel against your manmade, unjust, unconstitutional forms of law, that tax, fine, imprison and hang women, while they deny them the right of representation in the government; and I shall work on with might and main to pay every dollar of that honest debt, but not a penny shall go to this unjust claim. And I shall earnestly and persistently continue to urge all women to the practical recognition of the old revolutionary maxim, that 'Resistance to tyranny is obedience to God.'"

Judge Hunt, in a move calculated to preclude any appeal to a higher court, ended the trial by announcing, "Madam, the Court will not order you committed until the fine is paid."

No Fines Paid

True to her word, Anthony never paid a penny of her fine. Her petition to Congress to remit the fine was never acted upon, but no serious effort was ever made by the government to collect.

Anthony tried to turn her trial and conviction into political gains for the women suffrage movement. She ordered 3,000 copies of the trial proceedings printed and distributed them to political activists, politicians, and libraries. In the eyes of some, the trial had elevated Anthony to the status of the martyr, while for others the effect may have been to diminish her status to that of a common criminal. Many in the press, however, saw Anthony as the ultimate victor. One New York paper observed, "If it is a mere question of who got the best of it, Miss Anthony is still ahead. She has voted and the American constitution has survived the shock. Fining her one hundred dollars does not rule out the fact that . . . women voted, and went home, and the world jogged on as before."

Minor v. Happersett: The Fourteenth Amendment Does Not Give Women Voting Rights

Morrison R. Waite

The 1874 case Minor v. Happersett *was the only suit dealing with women's voting rights to reach the U.S. Supreme Court. The plaintiff, Virginia Minor, a suffragist from Missouri, alleged that the state's refusal to allow her to register to vote was an infringement on her civil rights under the "privileges and immunities clause" of the Fourteenth Amendment to the U.S. Constitution. In the following excerpt from the court's unanimous opinion, Chief Justice Morrison R. Waite discusses the definition of citizenship and explains the privileges and immunities granted to citizens according to the U.S. Constitution. In the Court's opinion, suffrage is not a privilege of citizenship and was not specifically intended by the Constitution's framers. Waite served as Chief Justice of the Supreme Court from 1874 to 1888.*

The question is presented in this case, whether, since the adoption of the fourteenth amendment, a woman, who is a citizen of the United States and of the State of Missouri, is a voter in that State, notwithstanding the provision of the constitution and laws of the State, which confine the right of suffrage to men alone. . . .

It is contended that the provisions of the constitution and laws of the State of Missouri which confine the right of suffrage and registration therefor to men, are in violation of the Constitution of the United States, and therefore void. The argument is, that as a woman, born or naturalized in the United States and subject to the jurisdiction thereof, is a citizen of the United States and of the State in which she resides, she has

U.S. Supreme Court, *Minor v. Happersett*, 1874.

the right of suffrage as one of the privileges and immunities of her citizenship, which the State cannot by its laws or constitution abridge.

There is no doubt that women may be citizens. They are persons, and by the fourteenth amendment 'all persons born or naturalized in the United States and subject to the jurisdiction thereof' are expressly declared to be 'citizens of the United States and of the State wherein they reside.' But, in our opinion, it did not need this amendment to give them that position. Before its adoption the Constitution of the United States did not in terms prescribe who should be citizens of the United States or of the several States, yet there were necessarily such citizens without such provision. There cannot be a nation without a people. The very idea of a political community, such as a nation is, implies an association of persons for the promotion of their general welfare. Each one of the persons associated becomes a member of the nation formed by the association. He owes it allegiance and is entitled to its protection. Allegiance and protection are, in this connection, reciprocal obligations. The one is a compensation for the other; allegiance for protection and protection for allegiance.

For convenience it has been found necessary to give a name to this membership. The object is to designate by a title the person and the relation he bears to the nation. For this purpose the words 'subject,' 'inhabitant,' and 'citizen' have been used, and the choice between them is sometimes made to depend upon the form of the government. Citizen is now more commonly employed, however, and as it has been considered better suited to the description of one living under a republican government, it was adopted by nearly all of the States upon their separation from Great Britain, and was afterwards adopted in the Articles of Confederation and in the Constitution of the United States. When used in this sense it is understood as conveying the idea of membership of a nation, and nothing more. . . .

Sex has never been made one of the elements of citizenship in the United States. In this respect men have never had an advantage over women. The same laws precisely apply to both. The fourteenth amendment did not affect the citizenship of women any more than it did of men. In this particular, therefore, the rights of Mrs. Minor do not depend upon the amendment. She has always been a citizen from her birth, and entitled to all the privileges and immunities of citizenship. The amendment prohibited the State, of which she is a citizen, from abridging any of her privileges and immunities as a citizen of the United States; but it did not confer citizenship on her. That she had before its adoption.

Determining Whether All Citizens Are Voters

If the right of suffrage is one of the necessary privileges of a citizen of the United States, then the constitution and laws of Missouri confining it to men are in violation of the Constitution of the United States, as amended, and consequently void. The direct question is, therefore, presented whether all citizens are necessarily voters.

The Constitution does not define the privileges and immunities of citizens. For that definition we must look elsewhere. In this case we need not determine what they are, but only whether suffrage is necessarily one of them.

It certainly is nowhere made so in express terms. The United States has no voters in the States of its own creation. The elective officers of the United States are all elected directly or indirectly by State voters. The members of the House of Representatives are to be chosen by the people of the States, and the electors in each State must have the qualifications requisite for electors of the most numerous branch of the State legislature. Senators are to be chosen by the legislatures of the States, and necessarily the members of the legislature required to make the choice are elected by the voters of the

State. Each State must appoint in such manner, as the legislature thereof may direct, the electors to elect the President and Vice-President. The times, places, and manner of holding elections for Senators and Representatives are to be prescribed in each State by the legislature thereof; but Congress may at any time, by law, make or alter such regulations, except as to the place of choosing Senators. It is not necessary to inquire whether this power of supervision thus given to Congress is sufficient to authorize any interference with the State laws prescribing the qualifications of voters, for no such interference has ever been attempted. The power of the State in this particular is certainly supreme until Congress acts.

The amendment did not add to the privileges and immunities of a citizen. It simply furnished an additional guaranty for the protection of such as he already had. No new voters were necessarily made by it. Indirectly it may have had that effect, because it may have increased the number of citizens entitled to suffrage under the constitution and laws of the States, but it operates for this purpose, if at all, through the States and the State laws, and not directly upon the citizen.

Suffrage Was Not Intended to Be a Privilege of Citizenship

It is clear, therefore, we think, that the Constitution has not added the right of suffrage to the privileges and immunities of citizenship as they existed at the time it was adopted. This makes it proper to inquire whether suffrage was coextensive with the citizenship of the States at the time of its adoption. If it was, then it may with force be argued that suffrage was one of the rights which belonged to citizenship, and in the enjoyment of which every citizen must be protected. But if it was not, the contrary may with propriety be assumed.

When the Federal Constitution was adopted, all the States, with the exception of Rhode Island and Connecticut, had constitutions of their own. These two continued to act under their charters from the Crown. Upon an examination of those constitutions we find that in no State were all citizens permitted to vote. Each State determined for itself who should have that power. Thus, in New Hampshire, 'every male inhabitant of each town and parish with town privileges, and places unincorporated in the State, of twenty-one years of age and upwards, excepting paupers and persons excused from paying taxes at their own request,' were its voters; in Massachusetts 'every male inhabitant of twenty-one years of age and upwards, having a freehold estate within the commonwealth of the annual income of three pounds, or any estate of the value of sixty pounds'; in Rhode Island 'such as are admitted free of the company and society' of the colony; in Connecticut such persons as had 'maturity in years, quiet and peaceable behavior, a civil conversation, and forty shillings freehold or forty pounds personal estate,' if so certified by the selectmen. . . .

In this condition of the law in respect to suffrage in the several States it cannot for a moment be doubted that if it had been intended to make all citizens of the United States voters, the framers of the Constitution would not have left it to implication. So important a change in the condition of citizenship as it actually existed, if intended, would have been expressly declared. But if further proof is necessary to show that no such change was intended, it can easily be found both in and out of the Constitution. By Article 4, section 2, it is provided that 'the citizens of each State shall be entitled to all the privileges and immunities of citizens in the several States.' If suffrage is necessarily a part of citizenship, then the citizens of each State must be entitled to vote in the several States precisely as their citizens are. This is more than asserting that they may change their residence and become citizens of the State and thus be voters. It goes to the extent of insisting that while retaining their original citizenship they may vote in any State. This, we think, has never been claimed. And again, by the very terms of the amendment we have been considering (the fourteenth), 'Representatives shall be apportioned among the several States according to their respective numbers, counting the whole number of persons in each State, excluding Indians not taxed. But when the right to vote at any election for the choice of electors for President and Vice-President of the United States, representatives in Congress, the executive and judicial officers of a State, or the members of the legislature thereof, is denied to any of the male inhabitants of such State, being twenty-one years of age and citizens of the United States, or in any way abridged, except for participation in the rebellion, or other crimes, the basis of representation therein shall be reduced in the proportion which the number of such male citizens shall bear to the whole number of male citizens twenty-one years of age in such State.' Why this, if it was not in the power of the legislature to deny the right of suffrage to some male inhabitants? And if suffrage was necessarily one of the absolute rights of citizenship, why confine the operation of the limitation to male inhabitants? Women and children are, as we have seen, 'persons.' They are counted in the enumeration upon which the apportionment is to be made, but if they were necessarily voters because of their citizenship unless clearly excluded, why inflict the penalty for the exclusion of males alone? Clearly, no such form of words would have been selected to express the idea here indicated if suffrage was the absolute right of all citizens.

And still again, after the adoption of the fourteenth amendment, it was deemed necessary to adopt a fifteenth, as follows: 'The right of citizens of the United States to vote shall not be denied or abridged by the United States, or by any State, on account of race, color, or previous condition of servitude.' The fourteenth amendment had already provided that no State should make or enforce any law which should abridge the privileges or immunities of citizens of the United States. If suffrage was one of these privileges or immunities, why amend the Constitution to prevent its being denied on account of race, [color, or previous condition of servitude]? Nothing is more evident than that the greater must include the less, and if all were already protected why go through with the form of amending the Constitution to protect a part?

Suffrage for Women Is Not Automatically Guaranteed by a Republican Form of Government

It is true that the United States guarantees to every State a republican form of government. It is also true that no State can pass a bill of attainder [a legislative act declaring a person guilty of a crime without a trial], and that no person can be deprived of life, liberty, or property without due process of law. All these several provisions of the Constitution must be construed in connection with the other parts of the instrument, and in the light of the surrounding circumstances.

The guaranty is of a republican form of government. No particular government is designated as republican, neither is the exact form to be guaranteed, in any manner especially designated. Here, as in other parts of the instrument, we are compelled to resort elsewhere to ascertain what was intended.

The guaranty necessarily implies a duty on the part of the States themselves to provide such a government. All the States had governments when the Constitution was adopted. In all the people participated to some extent, through their representatives elected in the manner specially provided. These governments the Constitution did not change. They were accepted precisely as they were, and it is, therefore, to be presumed that they were such as it was the duty of the States to provide. Thus we have unmistakable evidence of what was republican in form, within the meaning of that term as employed in the Constitution. As has been seen, all the citizens of the States were not invested with the right of suffrage. In all, save perhaps New Jersey, this right was only bestowed upon men and not upon all of them. Under these circumstances it is certainly now too late to contend that a government is not republican, within the meaning of this guaranty in the Constitution, because women are not made voters.

The same may be said of the other provisions just quoted. . . . So also of the amendment which declares that no person shall be deprived of life, liberty, or property without due process of law, adopted as it was as early as 1791. If suffrage was intended to be included within its obligations, language better adapted to express that intent would most certainly have been employed. The right of suffrage, when granted, will be protected. He who has it can only be deprived of it by due process of law, but in order to claim protection he must first show that he has the right.

But we have already sufficiently considered the proof found upon the inside of the Constitution. That upon the outside is equally effective.

Suffrage and the Constitution

The Constitution was submitted to the States for adoption in 1787, and was ratified by nine States in 1788, and finally by the thirteen original States in 1790. Vermont was the first new State admitted to the Union, and it came in under a constitution which conferred the right of suffrage only upon men of the full age of twenty-one years, having resided in the State for the space of one whole year next before the election, and who were of quiet and peaceable behavior. This was in 1791. The next year, 1792, Kentucky followed with a constitution confining the right of suffrage to free male citizens of the age of twenty-one years who had resided in the State two years or in the county in which they offered to vote one year next before the election. Then followed Tennessee, in 1796, with voters of freemen of the age of twenty-one years and upwards, possessing a freehold in the county wherein they may vote, and being inhabitants of the State or freemen being inhabitants of any one county in the State six months immediately preceding the day of election. But we need not particularize further. No new State has ever been admitted to the Union which has conferred the right of suffrage upon women, and this has never been considered a valid objection to her admission. On the contrary, as is claimed in the argument, the right of suffrage was withdrawn from women as early as 1807 in the State of New Jersey, without any attempt to obtain the interference of the United States to prevent it. Since then the governments of the insurgent States have been reorganized under a requirement that before their representatives could be admitted to seats in Congress they must have adopted new constitutions, republican in form. In no one of these constitutions was suffrage conferred upon women, and yet the States have all been restored to their original position as States in the Union.

Besides this, citizenship has not in all cases been made a condition precedent to the enjoyment of the right of suffrage. Thus, in Missouri, persons of foreign birth, who have declared their intention to become citizens of the United States, may under certain circumstances vote. The same provision is to be found in the constitutions of Alabama, Arkansas, Florida, Georgia, Indiana, Kansas, Minnesota, and Texas.

Certainly, if the courts can consider any question settled, this is one. For nearly ninety years the people have acted upon the idea that the Constitution, when it conferred citizenship, did not necessarily confer the right of suffrage. If uniform practice long continued can settle the construction of so important an instrument as the Constitution of the United States confessedly is, most certainly it has been done here. Our province is to decide what the law is, not to declare what it should be.

We have given this case the careful consideration its importance demands. If the law is wrong, it ought to be changed; but the power for that is not with us. The arguments addressed to us bearing upon such a view of the subject may perhaps be sufficient to induce those having the power, to make the alteration, but they ought not to be permitted to influence our judgment in determining the present rights of the parties now litigating before us. No argument as to woman's need of suffrage can be considered. We can only act upon her rights as they exist. It is not for us to look at the hardship of withholding. Our duty is at an end if we find it is within the power of a State to withhold.

The National Woman's Party Trials

Kathryn Cullen-DuPont

In June 1917, a number of suffragists picketing in front of the White House were arrested. In the following selection, Kathryn Cullen-DuPont describes the arrests and trials of Alice Paul, leader of the National Woman's Party, and other women. After more than fifty suffragists were arrested for obstructing sidewalks or obstructing traffic, Judge Alexander Mullowney considered using the Espionage Act of 1917 against the women. When this failed, all of the women were charged with obstructing traffic. Alice Paul was was sentenced to seven months' imprisonment. While incarcerated, she maintained a hunger strike and petitioned to be treated as a political prisoner. In November of that year, Cullen-DuPont explains, all of the imprisoned suffragists were released with no explanation. Cullen-DuPont graduated from New York University and has authored books and articles on women's history and women's rights.

Women first organized to demand suffrage in 1848, at what became known as the Seneca Falls Convention. In 1917, despite 69 years of active campaigning, women were still without the vote. Members of Alice Paul's National Woman's Party decided to try a new tactic, and on January 10 they began picketing President Woodrow Wilson and the White House.

Ignored by the Government

Prior to the United States' entrance into World War I, the women received no attention from the government. Shortly after the declaration of war, however, Alice Paul was warned

Kathryn Cullen-DuPont, "The Trials of Alice Paul and Other National Woman's Party Members: 1917," *Great American Trials*, Canton, MI: Visible Ink Press, 1994. Copyright © 1994 New England Publishing Associates, Inc. Reproduced by permission.

by the chief of police for the District of Columbia that picketers would now have to be arrested. Paul replied that her lawyers had "assured us all along that picketing was legal," and she maintained that it was "certainly . . . as legal in June as in January." The first two picketers were nonetheless arrested on June 22, 1917. They were charged with obstructing a sidewalk but released and never tried, as were 27 other women within the next four days. This process failed to put an end to the picketing, and on June 27 six women stood trial for obstructing traffic. They were found guilty and fined $25.00. Because they refused to pay their fine, they were sentenced to three days in jail.

The picketing continued. On July 14, 16 women were arrested, including Florence Bayard Hilles, the daughter of a former American ambassador to Great Britain, and Allison Turnbull Hopkins, the wife of President Wilson's New Jersey campaign coordinator. They stood trial the same day before district court Judge Alexander Mullowney.

Using the Espionage Act

Mullowney had earlier consulted the U.S. Attorney about the possibility of trying the women under the Espionage Act of 1917. Passed in June, it outlawed, among other things, the making of untrue statements which interfered with the conduct of war. The women's banners, Mullowney said, contained "words . . . [that] are treasonous and seditious." As it turned out, however, the women's banners contained what they considered ironic quotations of President Wilson's own speeches, such as a line from his War Message Speech of April 2: "WE SHALL FIGHT FOR THE THINGS WHICH WE HAVE ALWAYS HELD NEAREST OUR HEARTS—FOR DEMOCRACY, FOR THE RIGHT OF THOSE WHO SUBMIT TO AUTHORITY TO HAVE A VOICE IN THEIR OWN GOVERNMENTS." Since the president's own words could not feasibly be brought up under the Espionage Act, and because—as Paul had earlier

Social reformers Alice Paul and Lucy Burns, along with other suffragists as part of the National Woman's Party, picket the White House in 1917. The Library of Congress.

insisted—picketing was perfectly legal in the United States, the women were charged with the by-now expected "crime" of obstructing traffic. All 16 women were sentenced to 60 days in the Occoquan Workhouse.

A Presidential Pardon

A Wilson appointee and friend, Dudley Field Malone, collector of the Port of New York, happened to witness the women's trial. Outraged at its conclusion, he took a taxi to the White House and gave Wilson his resignation, stating that he planned to offer his legal services to the suffragists. Wilson refused to accept Malone's resignation. On July 20, the President pardoned all the suffragists imprisoned at Occoquan.

Picketing continued unabated, and arrests resumed in August. Dudley Field Malone offered his resignation again on September 7, this time forwarding copies of his letter to all the leading newspapers as well as to President Wilson, writing, "I think it is high time that men in this generation, at some cost to themselves, stood up to battle for the national enfranchisement of American women." This time, Malone's resignation was accepted.

Alice Paul Is Arrested

On October 4, Alice Paul herself was arrested along with 10 other women. In court October 8, the women refused to be sworn or to recognize the legitimacy of the court. Paul said: "We do not consider ourselves subject to this Court since, as an unenfranchised class, we have nothing to do with the making of the laws which have put us in this position." Although the charge was not dismissed, the women were released without sentence.

Alice Paul was arrested again on October 20, this time in the company of Dr. Caroline Spencer, Gladys Greiner, and Gertrude Crocker. The four were tried on October 22 before Judge Mullowney.

Police Sergeant Lee testified: "I made my way through the crowd that was surrounding them, and told the ladies they were violating the law by standing at the gates, and would not they please move on."

When Assistant District Attorney Hart asked Lee about the women's response, he replied: "They did not [move on], and they did not answer either ... [I] placed them under arrest."

Paul and Spencer, who had been carrying banners, were sentenced to seven months imprisonment. Greiner and Crocker, given the choice between $5.00 fines or 30 days imprisonment, elected to go to jail.

Political Prisoners

Lucy Burns, one of the first women arrested and released on June 22, had been arrested again in September and convicted; in Occoquan Workhouse before Paul's imprisonment, Burns organized the other incarcerated suffragists to request political prisoner status. Their petition was smuggled to the commissioners of the District of Columbia. Each of the signers was immediately placed in solitary confinement. At the end of October, Paul arrived at Occoquan with the recently sentenced

Rose Winslow, and the two announced a hunger strike to "secure for [their] fellow comrades treatment accorded political prisoners in every civilized country but our own."

Paul, Winslow, and others who joined the hunger strike were force-fed. Paul was held in solitary confinement and then transferred to a psychiatric hospital, where her windows were boarded over. Dudley Field Malone finally managed to have her released to a regular hospital on a writ of *habeas corpus*.

On November 27 and 28, 1917, all of the imprisoned suffragists were released without condition or explanation. On March 4, 1918, the District of Columbia Court of Appeals ruled on an appeal filed earlier by Malone. Each one of the suffragists had been "illegally arrested, illegally convicted, and illegally imprisoned."

The Nineteenth Amendment, enfranchising women, was adopted on August 26, 1920.

The Nebraska Referendum of 1919

James E. Potter

In 1917, Nebraska was on the verge of granting women's suffrage, as a legislative act gave women the right to vote in municipal and presidential elections. In the following essay, historian James Potter describes the battle between suffragists and antisuffragists in the aftermath of this act. Through petition drives, antisuffrage groups attempted to suspend women's voting rights until the issue could be put on the ballot for the November 1918 general election, certain that it would be defeated. Nebraska suffragists questioned the validity of the petitions and took the matter to court in the case Barkley v. Pool. *According to Potter, the suffragists gave evidence of improprieties in the petition-gathering effort, and the judge in the case prevented the antisuffragists from putting the issue on the ballot. This positive development for suffragists in Nebraska was soon overshadowed by total victory when the Nebraska legislature unanimously ratified the Nineteenth Amendment to the U.S. Constitution. Potter is the editor of* Nebraska History *magazine and a historian at the Nebraska State Historical Society.*

Nebraska suffragists had reason to rejoice when Governor Keith Neville, on April 21, 1917, signed a legislative act allowing women to vote in municipal elections and for presidential electors. Though not the full suffrage measure Nebraska women had been seeking, the law was a major breakthrough after decades of frustration and defeat. The legislature granted woman suffrage to the fullest extent possible under the state constitution, which continued to bar females from voting for most state officers. As the suffrage movement gained

James E. Potter, *"Barkley vs. Pool*: Woman Suffrage and the Nebraska Referendum Law," *Nebraska History*, vol. 69, Spring 1988, pp. 11–18. Reproduced by permission.

strength in Nebraska and elsewhere, it seemed likely that remaining constitutional barriers to full voting privileges for women would soon be eliminated.

Suffrage Law Suspended

A chill invaded this climate of optimism when it was learned that anti-suffrage forces planned to mount a referendum petition drive to force suspension of the new, limited suffrage law. After it became obvious that enough signatures had been gathered to suspend the law, the suffragists decided to seek an injunction to prevent the referendum from being placed on the ballot. During the next two years the Nebraska suffrage battle was waged in the courtroom. The case of *Barkley vs. Pool* eventually reached the Nebraska Supreme Court, which upheld a lower court ruling that the referendum petition drive had failed due to fraudulent and illegal procedures used in gathering signatures.

The decision in *Barkley vs. Pool* came too late to provide many opportunities for Nebraska women to vote. The suffrage law had been suspended while the case was in the courts. By the time the case was decided, the adoption of full suffrage amendments to the Nebraska and US constitutions was imminent. However, by discrediting the anti-suffrage forces, *Barkley vs. Pool* helped pave the way for the Nebraska Legislature's unanimous ratification of the federal suffrage amendment in August 1919. More importantly, the case demonstrated what appeared to be serious flaws in the statutes governing the initiative and referendum process. Because of the evidence presented by the suffragists in *Barkley vs. Pool*, the legislature in 1919 made more restrictive the legal requirements for circulating initiative or referendum petitions. . . .

The German-American Alliance

It was ironic that the groups seeking to prevent woman suffrage employed the referendum, which was a progressive reform anti-suffragists traditionally had opposed. No organiza-

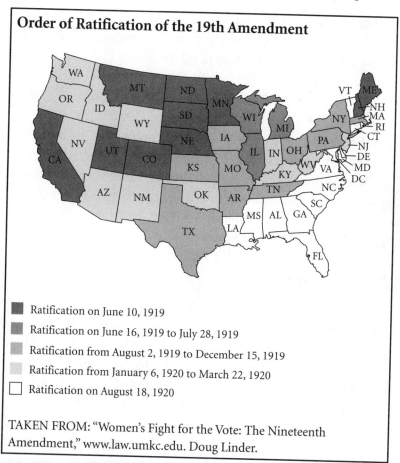

Order of Ratification of the 19th Amendment

■ Ratification on June 10, 1919

▨ Ratification on June 16, 1919 to July 28, 1919

▦ Ratification from August 2, 1919 to December 15, 1919

▫ Ratification from January 6, 1920 to March 22, 1920

□ Ratification on August 18, 1920

TAKEN FROM: "Women's Fight for the Vote: The Nineteenth Amendment," www.law.umkc.edu. Doug Linder.

tion was more hostile to woman suffrage than the German-American Alliance, whose opposition was related to ethnic and religious values. Not only did many German-Americans believe that a woman's place was in the home, but they feared that women voters would favor prohibition, a heartfelt issue for an ethnic group that generally regarded the drinking of alcoholic beverages as a matter of personal choice. The German-American Alliance was suspicious of the 1912 initiative and referendum amendments to the Nebraska constitution precisely because it feared that these constitutional weapons might be used by advocates of woman suffrage or prohibition to place such issues on the ballot.

The Alliance's fears were realized when an initiative petition drive succeeded in placing a woman suffrage amendment on the ballot for the 1914 general election. The anti-suffrage forces could not have felt much relief when the amendment lost by less than 10,000 votes. Compared to earlier elections where suffrage had been defeated four to one, the 1914 vote demonstrated that the suffrage movement was gaining momentum. Much worse was to come, however, when a prohibition amendment, added to the ballot by initiative in 1916, was approved in the general election by a majority of nearly 30,000 votes. Prohibition took effect on May 1, 1917, after the legislature passed enabling legislation.

War Leads to a Deal

Complicating the political situation for Nebraskans of German descent was the outbreak of war in Europe in 1914. As the ostensibly neutral United States moved closer to the Allied camp and war with Germany loomed, Nebraskans with ties to the fatherland sought to protect threatened cultural prerogatives, some of which had been confirmed by statute. One was the Mockett Law, which authorized foreign language instruction in the public schools. As anti-German sentiment increased in Nebraska, a movement to repeal the Mockett Law surfaced during the 1917 legislative session. This session, coinciding with American entry into the war, found the German-American members of the legislature increasingly on the defensive. In order to prevent repeal of the Mockett Law, German-stock lawmakers allegedly struck a deal to support the limited suffrage bill in return for votes from suffrage supporters to save the Mockett Law.

Others besides German-Americans had reason to fear woman suffrage and its implications for political reform. They included men like Omaha boss Tom Dennison, whose empire depended on bootlegging, gambling, and prostitution. The Dennison machine was already facing stiff opposition from

Omaha reformers without opening the voting booth to women. To people like Dennison, woman suffrage in municipal elections presented a clear threat to the political status quo.

Using the Referendum Process

After the 1917 legislature adjourned, a coalition of anti-suffrage forces made plans to defeat the limited suffrage law through the referendum process. If sufficient signatures could be gathered, the law would be suspended until it could be submitted to a vote of the people at the 1918 general election. Though there was no certainty that voters would reject the law, at least women would be barred from voting in the various municipal elections scheduled during the ensuing year and a half. . . .

Under the provisions of the 1913 referendum law, the anti-suffrage forces were required to gather 29,147 signatures within ninety days after the 1917 legislature adjourned in order to suspend the limited suffrage law for submission to a vote of the people. A group known as the Nebraska Association Opposed to Woman Suffrage, headquartered in Omaha, took the lead in the petition drive. This group allegedly was supported by various Omaha politicians, by the German-American Alliance, and by liquor interests. Probably for the sake of appearance, the organization's leadership included a number of women opposed to woman suffrage.

Newspapers Question Anti-Suffrage

Some newspapers questioned whether there was much support for the anti-suffrage position. The *Nebraska State Journal* doubted that 30,000 men would be willing to go on record in favor of depriving women of voting privileges already granted by the legislature. The newspaper castigated the anti-suffragist "diehards" for their efforts at a time when women were being "asked to fight for a country which will not grant them the responsibilities of citizenship." This sentiment was echoed by others including the editor of the *North Nebraska Eagle* of Dakota City:

> It should be known by anyone solicited to sign this petition that it has the legal effect of suspending the law for two years and is equivalent to denying to the women of Nebraska the small part in the government that the legislature gave them. If you believe in suffrage refuse to sign such a petition. It requires 30,000 names and the *Eagle* does not believe there are that many men in Nebraska who will openly declare themselves so unfair.

Despite observers' skepticism about the petition drive's chances for success, signatures were collected without apparent difficulty. On July 21, 1917, anti-suffrage leader Mrs. L.B. Crofoot, whose husband was president of the anti-prohibition "Prosperity League," presented petitions containing over 32,000 signatures to Secretary of State Charles W. Pool. The ease with which the signatures had been gathered aroused the suspicions of the Nebraska Woman Suffrage Association. Suffragists grew even more suspicious when newspapers reported that circulators had been paid for signatures gathered in Omaha pool halls and "soft drink" parlors, and that petition circulators had represented the petition as a pro-suffrage document.

After determining that the required number of signatures had been collected, the secretary of state announced his intention to place the referendum on the ballot for the November 1918 general election. The law did not require that he verify the validity of the petitions, stipulating only that he determine whether they contained enough signatures. Citizens who wished to challenge the petitions could, under the initiative and referendum statutes, seek an injunction against the secretary of state in Lancaster County District Court.

Mrs. Barkley Files Suit

On July 28, 1917, Mrs. Edna Barkley, president of the Nebraska Woman Suffrage Association, asked Secretary of State Pool for permission to examine the anti-suffrage petitions. At first Pool refused, offering to provide copies; later he gave representatives of the association free access to the petitions.

The suffragists planned to challenge the petitions on the basis of fraud. Because 18,000 of the more than 30,000 signatures were gathered in Omaha, it was there that they decided to concentrate their efforts. In September 1917 members of the association began working to verify names and addresses. By mid-February 1918 the suffragists were ready to go to court in an effort to prove that the referendum petition drive had failed.

On February 18 Mrs. Barkley and eighteen co-plaintiffs filed suit in Lancaster County District Court. They asked Judge Leonard A. Flansburg for an injunction against Secretary of State Pool to prevent Pool from placing the referendum on the November general election ballot. The suffragists charged that the petitions violated the referendum law in several respects. The suit argued that many of the signatures on the petitions were not genuine, that many petitions were certified illegally, that some circulators had engaged in fraud to procure signatures, and that altogether the referendum petitions did not contain the number of genuine signatures required by law.

On March 16 eighty-seven men and women active in the anti-suffrage ranks petitioned the court and were permitted to join the case as "intervenors." Judge Flansburg appointed a special examiner to take testimony regarding the authenticity of referendum petitions that had been circulated across the state. The suffragists, who had spent long hours investigating petition signatures in Omaha and elsewhere, were ready to present their evidence.

Petition Hearings Proceed

As the hearings proceeded, it became clear that a final ruling in the case might not be made before the November 1918 election. The anti-suffragists hoped the delay might force the issue to a vote of the people regardless of the ongoing investigation. To prevent the secretary of state from placing the referendum on the November ballot the plaintiffs requested a temporary restraining order against Pool. Judge Flansburg issued the order on July 6, 1918.

Throughout the summer and fall of 1918 the hearings dragged on. After being presented with convincing evidence that fraudulent signatures had been found on some of the petitions circulated in Omaha, Judge Flansburg decided to replace the restraining order with a temporary injunction against the secretary of state.

Checking Signatures

The suffragists used a process as simple as it was time consuming to check the validity of signatures. They copied petitions filed with the secretary of state and tried to verify each name and address. Some 18,000 names were checked in Omaha by suffrage workers under the leadership of Mrs. Katherine Sumney and Mrs. Grace Richardson. The workers found that many of the addresses on petitions were fictitious and that the localities named were in the middle of cornfields or railroad yards. Some addresses, had they existed, would have been located in the Missouri River. The suffragists discovered petitions bearing the names of men who had never lived at the addresses given and who, when contacted, affirmed that they had never signed any petition. Some men said that they had signed a petition because the circulator had represented it as a pro-suffrage petition; others thought it was a petition to "bring back beer." Paid circulators from Omaha traveled around the state collecting signatures. In at least one instance a circulator was a resident of Iowa. A person named

A.O. Barclay had certified to 112 Douglas County petitions on which many of the signatures could not be verified. Despite the efforts of investigators, Barclay was never located.

Handwriting experts testified that all signatures on many petitions were in the same handwriting. Other petitions were found to have been left in pool halls, cigar stores, and barber shops for anyone to sign. Some were circulated by minors or by illiterates who were paid a fee for each signature. In several instances, the plaintiffs proved that men whose signatures appeared on petitions had died months before the petitions were circulated. One Nebraska newspaper noted that "many dead and gone long before the suffrage question ever became an issue in Nebraska apparently returned to Earth to fight suffrage." . . .

One fact that was particularly galling to the suffragists was that many petition signers were not citizens. The Nebraska constitution provided that males who had declared their intention to become citizens (e.g. had taken out their "first papers") were "electors" and qualified to sign initiative or referendum petitions. It seemed poetic justice later when, just as the ruling in *Barkley vs. Pool* restored limited voting rights to women, a 1918 constitutional amendment prohibiting alien suffrage took effect, disenfranchising thousands who had never bothered to become citizens.

Temporary Injunction Becomes Permanent

In issuing the temporary injunction, Judge Flansburg ruled that the plaintiffs had proved that many of the names on specific petitions had been fraudulently written there by the circulators. Therefore those entire petitions would be disqualified unless the intervenors could prove that the remaining signatures were genuine. However, except for generally denying knowledge of any fraud, the anti-suffrage leaders made no effort to refute the testimony of the plaintiffs. They convinced

Judge Flansburg to issue a special finding that the Omaha women who directed the circulation of the petitions had not been shown to have been implicated in the frauds! After the temporary injunction was issued, the anti-suffrage forces appealed to the Nebraska Supreme Court, which refused to hear the appeal on the grounds that the district court injunction was not a final order in the case.

On January 24, 1919, Judge Flansburg issued a permanent injunction to prevent the secretary of state from submitting the limited suffrage law to a vote of the people. The judge found that fraud, forgery, and false certification invalidated more than 4,600 signatures on the referendum petitions and that the required number of valid signatures had not been collected. He assessed the costs in the case to the state (as defendant) and to the intervenors. The Nebraska attorney general ruled that women were eligible to vote in upcoming municipal elections under the provisions of the 1917 limited suffrage law.

The Injunction Is Appealed

On April 28 the intervenors appealed Judge Flansburg's ruling to the Nebraska Supreme Court while the state, having accepted the decision, withdrew from the case. The intervenors appealed on the grounds that the judge had erred in throwing out entire petitions when only certain names had been proved fraudulent, that the plaintiffs (who were not eligible to vote) had no right to sue because the suit pertained to a political, rather than a civil right; and that the injunction prevented the legal voters of the state from voting on the question of woman suffrage.

In upholding Judge Flansburg's ruling the [Nebraska] Supreme Court on June 28, 1919, agreed that the remedy of injunction against fraudulent referendum petitions was available to any citizen including non-voting women, and that knowingly certifying to a fraudulent signature on a referendum petition destroyed the credibility of the circulator to the degree that the entire petition was invalidated.

The Nineteenth Amendment Is Ratified

In the aftermath of this protracted struggle the suffrage movement soon achieved final victory. On August 2, 1919, the Nebraska legislature in special session unanimously ratified the nineteenth amendment to the US Constitution. After ratification by other states the federal amendment took effect in August 1920. A Nebraska constitutional convention proposed a full suffrage amendment to the state constitution, which was approved by the votes of both men and women at a September 21, 1920, special election. . . .

More than Suffrage

Though they could not yet vote, Nebraska suffragists made a significant contribution to Nebraska's political history through their fight against the referendum on the 1917 limited suffrage law. They demonstrated the fallacy of the anti-suffrage argument that women were "too delicate" for the rough and tumble world of politics. In order to protect a fundamental concept of direct democracy, they waged a lengthy and expensive legal battle more important in principle than for its eventual effect on the suffrage cause. By the time they won full suffrage, Nebraska women had already demonstrated that they were ready for, and capable of, full participation in the political process.

The Poll Tax Case:
Breedlove v. Suttles

Pierce Butler

In 1937 the U.S. Supreme Court heard its only case related to the Nineteenth Amendment. The case dealt with poll tax laws in the state of Georgia, assessing whether they were constitutional according to the voting privileges granted by the Fourteenth and Nineteenth Amendments. In the following majority opinion, Justice Pierce Butler outlines who is exempt from paying the poll tax. He also explains that the Nineteenth Amendment pertains to the right to vote and not to the collection of taxes. The Supreme Court affirmed the decision of the lower court to uphold the paying of poll taxes. Pierce Butler was a conservative justice who served on the Supreme Court from 1923 until 1939.

A Georgia statute provides that there shall be levied and collected each year from every inhabitant of the state between the ages of 21 and 60 a poll tax of one dollar, but that the tax shall not be demanded from the blind or from females who do not register for voting. The State Constitution declares that, to entitle a person to register and vote at any election, he shall have paid all poll taxes that he may have had opportunity to pay agreeably to law. The form of oath prescribed to qualify an elector contains a clause declaring compliance with that requirement. Tax collectors may not allow any person to register for voting unless satisfied that his poll taxes have been paid. Appellant brought this suit in the superior court of Fulton county to have the clause of the Constitution and the statutory provisions above mentioned declared repugnant to various provisions of the Federal Constitution and to compel appellee to allow him to register for voting without payment of poll taxes. The court dismissed his petition. The state Supreme Court affirmed.

U.S. Supreme Court, *Breedlove v. Suttles*, 302 U.S. 277, 1937.

Supreme Court Justice Pierce Butler wrote the majority opinion in Breedlove v. Suttles, *explaining that the Nineteenth Amendment pertains to the right to vote and not to the collection of poll taxes.* The Library of Congress.

The pertinent facts alleged in the petition are these. March 16, 1936, appellant, a white male citizen 28 years old, applied to appellee to register him for voting for federal and state officers at primary and general elections. He informed appellee he had neither made poll tax returns nor paid any poll taxes, and had not registered to vote because a receipt for poll taxes and an oath that he had paid them are prerequisites to registration. He demanded that appellee administer the oath, omitting the part declaring payment of poll taxes, and allow him to register. Appellee refused.

Appellant maintains that the provisions in question are repugnant to the equal protection clause and the privileges and immunities clause of the Fourteenth Amendment, and to the Nineteenth Amendment.

The Rule of Equality

1. He asserts that the law offends the rule of equality in that it extends only to persons between the ages of 21 and 60 and to women only if they register for voting, and in this it makes payment a prerequisite to registration. He does not suggest that exemption of the blind is unreasonable.

Levy by the poll has long been a familiar form of taxation, much used in some countries and to a considerable extent here at first in the colonies and later in the states. To prevent burdens deemed grievous and oppressive, the Constitutions of some states prohibit or limit poll taxes. That of Georgia prevents more than a dollar a year. Poll taxes are laid upon persons without regard to their occupations or property to raise money for the support of government or some more specific end. The equal protection clause does not require absolute equality. While possible by statutory declaration to levy a poll tax upon every inhabitant of whatsoever sex, age, or condition, collection from all would be impossible, for always there are many too poor to pay. Attempt equally to enforce such a measure would justify condemnation of the tax as harsh and unjust. Collection from minors would be to put the burden upon their fathers or others upon whom they depend for support. It is not unreasonable to exclude them from the class taxed.

Men who have attained the age of 60 are often, if not always, excused from road work, jury duty and service in the militia. They have served or have been liable to be called on to serve the public to the extent that the state chooses to require. So far as concerns equality under the equal protection clause, there is no substantial difference between these exemptions and exemption from poll taxes. The burden laid upon appellant is precisely that put upon other men. The rate is a dollar a year, commencing at 21 and ending at 60 years of age.

The tax being upon persons, women may be exempted on the basis of special considerations to which they are naturally entitled. In view of burdens necessarily borne by them for the preservation of the race, the state reasonably may exempt them from poll taxes. The laws of Georgia declare the husband to be the head of the family and the wife to be subject to him. To subject her to the levy would be to add to his burden. Moreover, Georgia poll taxes are laid to raise money for educational purposes, and it is the father's duty to provide for education of the children. Discrimination in favor of all women being permissible, appellant may not complain because the tax is laid only upon some or object to registration of women without payment of taxes for previous years.

Payment as a prerequisite is not required for the purpose of denying or abridging the privilege of voting. It does not limit the tax to electors; aliens are not there permitted to vote, but the tax is laid upon them, if within the defined class. It is not laid upon persons 60 or more years old, whether electors or not. Exaction of payment before registration undoubtedly serves to aid collection from electors desiring to vote, but that use of the state's power is not prevented by the Federal Constitution.

2. To make payment of poll taxes a prerequisite of voting is not to deny any privilege or immunity protected by the Fourteenth Amendment. Privilege of voting is not derived from the United States, but is conferred by the state and, save

as restrained by the Fifteenth and Nineteenth Amendments and other provisions of the Federal Constitution, the state may condition suffrage as it deems appropriate. The privileges and immunities protected are only those that arise from the Constitution and laws of the United States, and not those that spring from other sources.

3. The Nineteenth Amendment, adopted in 1920, declares: "The right of citizens of the United States to vote shall not be denied or abridged by the United States or by any State on account of sex." It applies to men and women alike and by its own force supersedes inconsistent measures, whether federal or state. Its purpose is not to regulate the levy or collection of taxes. The construction for which appellant contends would make the amendment a limitation upon the power to tax. The payment of poll taxes as a prerequisite to voting is a familiar and reasonable regulation long enforced in many states and for more than a century in Georgia. That measure reasonably may be deemed essential to that form of levy. Imposition without enforcement would be futile. Power to levy and power to collect are equally necessary. And, by the exaction of payment before registration, the right to vote is neither denied nor abridged on account of sex. It is fanciful to suggest that the Georgia law is a mere disguise under which to deny or abridge the right of men to vote on account of their sex. The challenged enactment is not repugnant to the Nineteenth Amendment.

Current Debates
on Equality
and Voting Rights

Guaranteeing the Right to Vote

John Bonifaz

In the following viewpoint, John Bonifaz argues that there are valid reasons for having a constitutional amendment guaranteeing the right to vote. Bonifaz notes that, as of 2005, there were 13,000 different voting standards in use in the Unites States. The U.S. Supreme Court has had a large say in previous voting debates, going against what Bonifaz believes are the basic principles of the U.S. Constitution. According to the author, reframing the Constitution to focus on voting rights is an important next step in our democracy. Bonifaz is founder of the National Voting Rights Institute, a nonprofit, nonpartisan organization that seeks to protect all citizens' voting rights.

In his new book, *don't think of an elephant!*, cognitive linguist George Lakoff discusses the importance of reframing for social change work.

"Frames," he says, "are mental structures that shape the way we see the world. As a result, they shape the goals we seek, the plans we make, the way we act, and what counts as a good or bad outcome of our actions. In politics our frames shape our social policies and the institutions we form to carry out policies. To change our frames is to change all of this. Reframing *is* social change."

Too Many Voting Standards

By proposing to amend the United States Constitution to guarantee the right to vote, we are engaged in the process of reframing the way we see our current political system. What does our right to vote mean today? Is it protected in our Con-

John Bonifaz, "A New Frame—A New Constitutional Amendment." www.nvri.org, March 31, 2005. Reproduced by permission. www.nvri.org/updates/bonifaz_remarks_au_conference_033105.pdf.

Civil rights marchers protest in front of the White House, leading up to passage of the Voting Rights Act in 1965. National Archive/Newsmakers/Getty Images.

stitution? Why do 108 democratic nations in the world have explicit language guaranteeing the right to vote in their constitutions, and the United States—along with only ten other such nations—does not? How can we claim to have an equal right to vote when the way we administer our elections changes from state to state, from county to county, from locality to locality? Thirteen thousand different systems. Thirteen thousand different standards.

A proposed constitutional amendment to guarantee the right to vote serves as a critical vehicle for creating a national dialogue in this country on the state of our right to vote and the state of our democracy. The nation has just witnessed another presidential election tainted by voter disenfranchisement, voter suppression, and widespread irregularities in the counting of the votes. Millions of citizens believe that this [2004 presidential] election, like the 2000 election, was not free and fair. A crisis of public confidence underlies the crisis in our democracy. This is a moment in history. Our response must go to the foundation of our political system: the US

Constitution—that social contract between we the people and our government, that supreme legal document which establishes the consent by which we agree to be governed.

Bush v. Gore and Other Supreme Court Cases

On December 12, 2000, this nation watched as the Supreme Court, for the first time in our history, stopped the counting of the votes and selected the president of the United States. In that ruling, *Bush v. Gore*, a 5–4 majority of the Court stated that the "individual citizen has no federal Constitutional right to vote for electors for President of the United States . . ." The right, the Court held, emanated from the states. Justice John Paul Stevens, one of the four dissenting justices, wrote, in his dissent, of the damage the ruling would inflict on "the Nation's confidence in the judge as an impartial guardian of the rule of law."

The *Bush v. Gore* ruling is not the only decision in Supreme Court jurisprudence that contravened [went against] the basic principles of our Constitution and our democracy. The nation's highest court has, unfortunately, done that before. *Dred Scott v. Sandford* (denying citizenship to all people of African ancestry and thereby upholding slavery), *Plessy v. Ferguson* (upholding the "separate but equal" doctrine), and *Korematsu v. United States* (upholding the internment of Japanese-Americans during World War II) are among the Court's rulings that belong on that list.

In the context of this constitutional amendment discussion, let us consider one such ruling and the history of how it eventually was overturned.

The Poll Tax Challenge

In 1937, the Supreme Court heard a constitutional challenge to the one-dollar poll tax in the state of Georgia, a fee charged to voters in order to vote and a barrier which existed throughout the Deep South. The Supreme Court in that case, *Breedlove v. Suttles*, upheld the poll tax as constitutional. "The payment of poll taxes as a prerequisite to voting," the Court ruled, "is a familiar and reasonable regulation long enforced in many States and for more than a century in Georgia." "Privilege of voting," the Court stated, "is not derived from the United States, but is conferred by the state and, save as restrained by the Fifteenth and Nineteenth Amendments and other provisions of the Federal Constitution, the state may condition suffrage as it deems appropriate."

In 1939, two years after the *Breedlove* ruling, an effort began in the US Congress to eliminate the poll tax in federal elections via a constitutional amendment. The effort would take a quarter of a century.

In the interim, the Court, in 1951, would hear a second challenge to the poll tax (*Butler v. Thompson*) and, once again, would uphold the poll tax as constitutional.

Then, from 1962–1964, in the heat of the Civil Rights Movement, Congress passed and the states ratified the Twenty-Fourth Amendment to the US Constitution, forever banning poll taxes in our federal elections.

Reversing a Precedent

That same year that ratification was completed for the Twenty-Fourth Amendment, Annie Harper and a group of poor Virginia voters with her challenged Virginia's poll tax in state elections. By the time her case reached the Supreme Court two years later, there remained four Southern states that held onto the poll tax for their state elections. And Virginia was one of them.

The Supreme Court's landmark 1966 ruling in *Harper v. Virginia Board of Elections*, reversing its own precedent and striking down the poll tax as unconstitutional, must be seen in concert with the Twenty-Fourth Amendment. While the majority opinion did not reference the amendment, Justice

John [Marshall] Harlan did in his dissent, calling the Court's abolition of the poll tax in state elections a "coup de grace. . . ." "Property qualifications and poll taxes have been a traditional part of our political structure," Harlan wrote.

> It is certainly a rational argument that payment of some minimal poll tax promotes civic responsibility, weeding out those who do not care enough about public affairs to pay $1.50 or thereabouts a year for the exercise of the franchise. It is also arguable . . . that people with some property have a deeper stake in community affairs, and are consequently more responsible, more educated, more knowledgeable, more worthy of confidence, than those without means, and that the community and Nation would be better managed if the franchise were restricted to such citizens.

But the majority in the *Harper* ruling recognized that the Court had been wrong in its 1937 and 1951 rulings upholding the poll tax and that the nation had progressed since that time. The ratification of the Twenty-Fourth Amendment, clearly in the minds of the justices, provided key evidence of this progress.

"[T]he Equal Protection Clause," Justice William O. Douglas wrote for the majority, "is not shackled to the political theory of a particular era. In determining what lines are unconstitutionally discriminatory, we have never been confined to historic notions of equality . . . Notions of what constitute equal treatment for purposes of the Equal Protection Clause do change."

"[W]ealth or fee paying," Justice Douglas continued, "has, in our view, no relation to voting qualifications; the right to vote is too precious, too fundamental to be so burdened or conditioned."

Change the Frame Again

The poll tax story is a story of reframing and the Twenty-Fourth Amendment played a crucial role in changing the frame. Today, a proposed constitutional amendment to guarantee the right to vote—to preserve the franchise with affirmative language in the Constitution—provides the nation with a powerful opportunity to change the frame for our time and to help move us toward the democracy that we promise to be.

The Perception of Women in Politics

Gloria Steinem

In the following viewpoint, Gloria Steinem argues that, in politics, being a woman is still a drawback. Discussing the differences between the racial barrier and the sex barrier, she points out what she sees as double standards in the treatment of Senators Hillary Clinton and Barack Obama by the media and voters during the 2008 presidential primary campaign. Steinem is a well-known feminist and women's rights advocate. She is the founder of Ms. *magazine and cofounder of the Women's Media Center.*

The woman in question became a lawyer after some years as a community organizer, married a corporate lawyer and is the mother of two little girls, ages 9 and 6. Herself the daughter of a white American mother and a black African father—in this race-conscious country, she is considered black— she served as a state legislator for eight years, and became an inspirational voice for national unity.

Be honest: Do you think this is the biography of someone who could be elected to the United States Senate? After less than one term there, do you believe she could be a viable candidate to head the most powerful nation on earth?

The Gender Question

If you answered no to either question, you're not alone. Gender is probably the most restricting force in American life, whether the question is who must be in the kitchen or who could be in the White House. This country is way down the

Gloria Steinem, "Women Are Never Frontrunners," *New York Times*, January 8, 2008. Reprinted with permission. www.nytimes.com/2008/01/08/opinion/08steinem.html.

Gloria Steinem is a women's advocate and founder of Ms. *magazine.* AP Images.

list of countries electing women and, according to one study, it polarizes gender roles more than the average democracy.

That's why the Iowa primary was following our historical pattern of making change. Black men were given the vote a half-century before women of any race were allowed to mark a ballot, and generally have ascended to positions of power, from the military to the boardroom, before any women (with the possible exception of obedient family members in the latter).

If the lawyer described above had been just as charismatic but named, say, Achola Obama instead of Barack Obama, her goose would have been cooked long ago. Indeed, neither she nor Hillary Clinton could have used Mr. Obama's public style—or Bill Clinton's either—without being considered too emotional by Washington pundits.

The Sex Barrier Versus the Racial Barrier

So why is the sex barrier not taken as seriously as the racial one? The reasons are as pervasive as the air we breathe: because sexism is still confused with nature as racism once was; because anything that affects males is seen as more serious than anything that affects "only" the female half of the human race; because children are still raised mostly by women (to put it mildly) so men especially tend to feel they are regressing to childhood when dealing with a powerful woman; because racism stereotyped black men as more "masculine" for so long that some white men find their presence to be masculinity-affirming (as long as there aren't too many of them); and because there is still no "right" way to be a woman in public power without being considered a you-know-what.

I'm not advocating a competition for who has it toughest. The caste systems of sex and race are interdependent and can only be uprooted together. That's why Senators Clinton and Obama have to be careful not to let a healthy debate turn into the kind of hostility that the news media love. Both will need a coalition of outsiders to win a general election. The abolition and suffrage movements progressed when united and were damaged by division; we should remember that.

How the Candidates Are Viewed

I'm supporting Senator Clinton because like Senator Obama she has community organizing experience, but she also has more years in the Senate, an unprecedented eight years of on-the-job training in the White House, no masculinity to prove, the potential to tap a huge reservoir of this country's talent by her example, and now even the courage to break the no-tears rule. I'm not opposing Mr. Obama; if he's the nominee, I'll volunteer. Indeed, if you look at votes during their two-year overlap in the Senate, they were the same more than 90 percent of the time. Besides, to clean up the mess left by President [George W.] Bush, we may need two terms of President Clinton and two of President Obama.

Many Different Worries

But what worries me is that he is seen as unifying by his race while she is seen as divisive by her sex.

What worries me is that she is accused of "playing the gender card" when citing the old boys' club, while he is seen as unifying by citing civil rights confrontations.

What worries me is that male Iowa voters were seen as gender-free when supporting their own, while female voters were seen as biased if they did and disloyal if they didn't.

What worries me is that reporters ignore Mr. Obama's dependence on the old—for instance, the frequent campaign comparisons to John F. Kennedy—while not challenging the slander that [Senator Clinton's] progressive policies are part of the Washington status quo.

What worries me is that some women, perhaps especially younger ones, hope to deny or escape the sexual caste system; thus Iowa women over 50 and 60, who disproportionately supported Senator Clinton, proved once again that women are the one group that grows more radical with age.

This country can no longer afford to choose our leaders from a talent pool limited by sex, race, money, powerful fathers and paper degrees. It's time to take equal pride in breaking all the barriers. We have to be able to say: "I'm supporting her because she'll be a great president and because she's a woman."

The Electoral College Should Be Abolished

The Rest of Us

In the following viewpoint, a political group argues that the U.S. Electoral College should be abolished because the reasons for establishing it in the first place no longer exist. The authors ask and answer questions about attempts to change the Electoral College, its role in small states, and its use in voting recounts. The authors also cover the requirement that the U.S. Constitution be amended in order to abolish the Electoral College. The Rest of Us is a political organization focused on the role of money in the political process.

Frequently asked questions about the Electoral College:

Why do we have the Electoral College in the first place?

The framers of the U.S. Constitution arrived at the Electoral College as a compromise between those who wanted direct popular election and those who wanted Congress to elect the President. They still saw our young nation as a collective of independent states, so they created a process of electing the nation's leader which reflected that view.

Also, the framers were concerned that voters would not have enough access to sufficient information about the candidates to make an informed decision, and that voters would generally vote exclusively for a candidate from their state, thereby weakening the cohesiveness of the young nation.

"Abolish the Electoral College: Let's Graduate to a Real Democracy," TheRestofUs.org, 2005. Reproduced by permission.

Concerns and Change

Don't those concerns still exist?

Basically, no. The United States has matured into a great united country over the last 200 years, with national interests and beliefs that cross all state boundaries. We go to war and pay taxes as a country, we should vote as a country too.

Newspapers, television, radio, and the internet all provide American citizens with enormous opportunities to become informed about the presidential candidates. We are now just as well informed as the electors we vote for, so there is no need to have intermediaries to cast votes on our behalf.

Regional differences may still exist, but a candidate's home state is not a guarantee of the votes of even his or her home state, as Al Gore and the people of Tennessee will attest. Americans vote for the president they think will do the best job, not the one that hails from a particular state.

What efforts have been made to change the Electoral College?

Several attempts have been made to get rid of the Electoral College, the last significant effort coming in 1969, when the House of Representatives passed 338–70 an amendment abolishing the Electoral College. The amendment died when it only received 54 votes in the Senate, 13 short of the required two-thirds. While this effort was ultimately unsuccessful, the overwhelming vote in the House shows that getting such an amendment passed is possible. Adding further proof that such an amendment is not only possible, but is favored by the great majority of Americans, a 1966 Gallup poll found that 63% of Americans favored a direct [election] of the president; a 2000 poll found that 61% did.

Doesn't the Electoral College contribute to the unity of the country by requiring a distribution of popular support to be elected president?

No. The Electoral College actually undermines the cohesiveness of the country by creating the possibility of minority rule over the majority and by creating a system of safe states and swing states. A system which encourages the presidential campaigns to ignore two-thirds of the country is hardly one which contributes to our country's unity.

Small States Versus Large States

But doesn't the Electoral College ensure that presidential candidates must pay attention to small states?

Because a state's representation in the U.S. House of Representatives is determined by its population in the census, larger states have more votes in the Electoral College than small states. However, small states end up having a greater representation in the Electoral College per capita than larger states because of the two electoral votes allotted for each state's Senators, which are not linked to population. Thus, Wyoming has one electoral vote per 164,592 residents, while California has one electoral vote per 627,253 people. This creates a situation in which a person standing on the Delaware side of the Delaware river has more than double the say of a person standing on the New Jersey side in who gets elected president.

Supporters of the Electoral College point to this as evidence that the Electoral College is working, that small states are protected from the large states. A look at the electoral map in the United States debunks this theory. We are no longer a nation in which the political divide runs along the lines of small states and large states, but one in which California, Delaware, and Maryland go one way and Texas, Georgia, and South Dakota go another.

The small-state/large-state argument is an anachronism. The truth is that the United States is a much more cohesive nation now than it was 200 years ago. We are attacked as a nation, not as a group of states. We go to war as a nation, not as a group of states. We pay taxes as a nation, not as a group of states. In picking the president, the person who would lead us on all these issues, we should vote as a nation too.

Recounts

What about recounts? Doesn't the Electoral College make it easier to do recounts?

It might, but a better way to solve the problem of recounts is to make sure up front that all eligible voters are registered and that their votes are cast and counted correctly. It's also the case that the popular vote winner could be quite clear in some elections, but the electoral vote quite close, thus requiring recounts in some states, as with Florida in 2000.

The Electoral College and the Constitution

Wouldn't abolishing the Electoral College require amending the Constitution?

Yes. Abolishing the Electoral College requires a constitutional amendment, which by design is not an easy thing to do: any amendment must pass two-thirds of both houses of Congress, after which three-fourths of the states must agree to it.

Shouldn't we defer to the framers of the Constitution when it comes to our elections?

Absolutely not. Despite the wisdom of the framers in crafting the U.S. Constitution, Americans have amended the Constitution five times to correct problems or unfairness relating to voting or our elections, including the following amendments: 15th—government can't deny the vote to a person based on color (minority suffrage); 17th—popular election of Senators; 19th—government can't deny the vote to a person based on gender (women's suffrage); 24th—no poll tax; 26th—18 year olds can vote.

The framers recognized that values and people change; that's why they created a process by which the Constitution could be changed. In the same way Americans changed the Constitution to reflect our beliefs that women and minorities must be allowed to vote, that we can handle the responsibility of electing our Senators, or that paying a tax to vote is un-American, we should change the Constitution to place the responsibility of electing our president directly on the shoulders of the American people.

The Electoral College Should Be Retained

Kevin R.C. Gutzman

In the following selection, Kevin R.C. Gutzman argues that the Electoral College should remain in place in the United States. Gutzman notes that America was set up as a republic. He explains the difference between national and federal and why the distinction is so important. He goes on to outline why the Electoral College is part of our voting system and why it should be retained, and concludes by offering a solution for making voting more equal. Gutzman, author of The Politically Incorrect Guide to the Constitution, *is an associate professor of history at Western Connecticut State University.*

In the wake of the 2000 presidential election, numerous commentators discovered what they took to be flaws in the presidential election system. For Hillary Clinton, for example, the election of George W. Bush demonstrated that the Electoral College should be abolished in favor of a French-style national election on a one-man, one-vote basis. Displaying her characteristic combination of ideological commitment and historical ignorance, Clinton opined that it simply was not right that the victory should go not to the recipient of the most popular votes, but to the winner in the Electoral College.

Writing in the *Claremont Review of Books* for Fall 2007, the University of Texas School of Law's Prof. Sanford Levinson takes up the same issue. Levinson, a prominent liberal legal academic who was once my Professional Responsibility professor, concedes that "I myself would endorse deviations from pure majoritarianism [the idea that the majority of the population has the right to make decisions for the entire popula-

Kevin R.C. Gutzman, "Beyond the Electoral College," LewRockwell.com, October 29, 2007. Reproduced by permission of the publisher and the author. www.lewrockwell.com.

tion]." He then offers as an example of a non-majoritarian provision of the federal Constitution so contrary to majoritarian theory that no one supports it: the provision for deciding presidential elections in which no one receives a majority of the Electoral College vote.

According to the Twelfth Amendment, "if no person have such majority, then from the persons having the highest numbers not exceeding three on the list of those voted for as President, the House of Representatives shall choose immediately, by ballot, the President, the votes shall be taken by states, the representation from each state having one vote." After describing this provision, Levinson says, "I have yet to find any defenders of the electoral college who are willing to defend this peculiar feature of the system."

Defense of the House of Representatives

Ah, Sandy, but you never asked me. I can defend the House's role in resolving presidential elections in which no one receives an Electoral College majority as easily as the veto power or bicameralism [a two-chamber legislative system], and certainly far more easily than universal suffrage or judicial review. And what, exactly, is wrong with it? Levinson's objection is that in case the House had to decide the issue with each state casting one vote, "Vermont's single representative [would have] the same power as California's 53 representatives."

This objection echoes Thomas Jefferson's objection to the apportionment provision of the 1776 Virginia Constitution. George Mason's handiwork retained the traditional English, thus colonial Virginian, practice of apportioning the legislature geographically. Thus, Jefferson complained, an individual's vote in Virginia's least populous county was worth seventeen times as much as an individual's vote in the most populous.

Different Objections

Yet, Levinson's objection and Jefferson's are not the same at all. Jefferson's complaint was that fellow citizens of a common republic (Virginia) should have equal votes in elections for their chief executive, while Levinson's is that the constituent republics in a federal republic, the states, should not have equal voices in choosing their common chief executive.

Levinson, like Senator Clinton, makes the mistake of thinking of the United States of America as a nation, not a federal republic. In Senator Clinton's defense, she likely has been influenced to reach that conclusion by "experts" such as Professor Levinson. On the other hand, Clinton's conclusion is affected by the fact that she desires the power of a national chief executive, not a mere federal president.

National Versus Federal

What is the difference between "national" and "federal," and why should you care? In short, a national government is, theoretically, a completely centralized one. If it has local subdivisions, those subdivisions (provinces) exist solely for the convenience of the center. This is the kind of regime that France has had since the French Revolution.

On the other hand, a federal regime is one in which the central government's power is limited, with most power remaining in the local units (in America, the states). The United States Constitution was sold to the states during the ratification process as a federal one. It could not have been ratified on any other basis, since the Revolution had been fought in the name of the federal model outlined by Thomas Jefferson in *A Summary View of the Rights of British America* (1774). The national model, in which a central government was sovereign (that is, possessed of unlimited power), was the one the British Parliament adopted in the hated Declaratory Act (1766).

In that act of 1766, the British Parliament claimed to be the kind of national government adored by such as Mrs. Clinton and Professor Levinson. In such a system, it makes sense that a national poll should be taken and the candidate with the most votes should be elected. Where the electorate is understood as made up of distinct communities, of different states that preexisted the federal constitution, however, it makes sense that those communities should have equal voices in making the ultimate decision. In other words, the Twelfth Amendment followed naturally from the assumptions behind the American Revolution.

The Electoral College as a Filter

Some scholars posit that the Electoral College was expected to serve only as a filter of popular opinion, and that Congress would usually decide among the three top candidates who had been essentially nominated by the College. The advantage of such a system would be that people more knowledgeable of the candidates' personalities, of their characters, would choose among them. A Bill Clinton, a Gary Hart, or a Richard Nixon would be unlikely to be elected in such an arena—or at least, so the argument goes. It would have pleased the father of the Electoral College, Luther Martin of Maryland, to have small states play an equal role in the ultimate selection of presidents.

Becoming Less Federal

Levinson wants to make the United States Government more national—less federal—by depriving the small states of their equal voices in the presidential election system. This reform would be typical of the history of the American Constitution: the small states and minority section were promised a federal system, and over time the majority section and the judges (egged on by such as Sanford Levinson) have made it more national. And they have done so while telling the minority that it had no choice but to succumb. All of which has made the system both theoretically and practically a worse system than it was originally.

If it is problematic that individual Californians' votes count less in the Senate, in the Electoral College, and in the occasional House of Representatives voting for president than those of Wyoming citizens, the solution is easy to identify: California should be divided into numerous less populous states. If it were, its citizens' and former citizens' votes would count more than they do now. The subdivision of megastates such as California should occur anyway, for numerous reasons—but that is a different column.

Women Are Still Not Equal

Lis Wiehl

In the following viewpoint, Lis Wiehl argues that even though women make up 51 percent of the U.S. population, they still have a long way to go to be equal with men. While women have made great strides since achieving the right to vote, only thirty-four women have served in the U.S. Senate, compared to more than 1,800 men. Wiehl discusses how women have both achieved success and been the targets of repression during the past sixty years. She questions why women have become less worried about their rights and less focused on protecting those rights for future generations. Wiehl is a trial lawyer and legal commentator, as well as an associate professor at the University of Washington School of Law.

It seems we have come a long way, baby. Commercials now hark that "choosy moms (and dads!) choose Jif!" And a woman has been president of the United States (at least on TV, until she got canceled). But is it only superficial? Are we just being pacified, yet still being served the same stale rap? Did we make some progress only to have it usurped while we were minding the kids? Have we taken two steps forward and one step back? Or worse . . . one step forward and two steps back?

True, we're no longer stuck in the narrow role of the middle-class American housewife that Betty Friedan described in *The Feminine Mystique*—certainly we'll all admit the women on *Desperate Housewives* are far from that—nor do we as a group feel harassed by the implied inequality of men holding doors for us. But are we treated equally under the law? Quite simply, *no!*

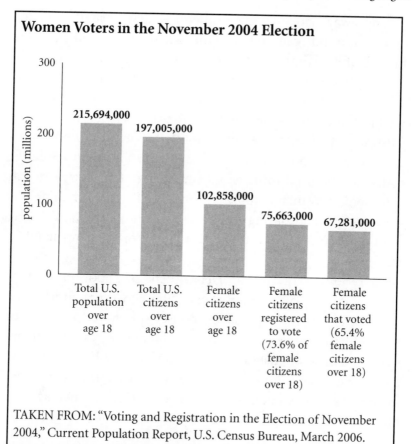

Women Voters in the November 2004 Election

TAKEN FROM: "Voting and Registration in the Election of November 2004," Current Population Report, U.S. Census Bureau, March 2006.

The Pink-Collar Problem

Women in America have fought for and achieved certain rights, such as the right to own property, the right to vote, and even the right to hold public office, but there's still gross inequity. For example, since 1789 only 34 women have served in the U.S. Senate, compared to 1,850 men. In the workplace, the pink-collar ghetto is alive and well. Though today we earn more than half of all bachelor's degrees, once out in the work-force we are still only making 73 cents for every dollar a man makes, and of the Fortune 500 companies, there are only eight women in the top positions. Our bodies are a veritable battle-ground, and not just over abortion. Several employers are now getting away with making women's weight part of their job description, but can you imagine a man being told he'd lose his job if he went bald? The average weight for women in their forties is twenty-five pounds heavier than it was in 1960, yet the "healthy" image from magazines is a look roughly twenty-five pounds lighter than it was then. Perhaps more frustrating is that we are continuously bombarded with stories and tricks on "how not to look fat" and more than a quarter of us feel the need to lie about our weight. Socially, we're still considered less than completely feminine if we're anything but demure—it's still daring to ask a man on a date, and downright audacious even to think of asking a man for his hand in marriage.

A recent survey by the Department of Labor shows that the average workingwoman spends about twice as much time as the average workingman on household chores and care of the children. On real estate deeds in many states, an unmarried woman is still listed as a "spinster." Funny how there isn't a male equivalent. And if you're not irritated yet, why is it that in many states women are denied prescription coverage for birth control even though men are allowed it for Viagra?

The Short End of the Stick

Yes, even with the drastic changes that have occurred in our society during the last twenty-five years, women still get . . . the short end of the stick.

This is nothing new. Throughout the centuries, women have consistently gotten the short end of the stick when it came to freedom, power, and property. In some times and places, this was sugarcoated with idealization—women were pure, dainty creatures who ought not soil their pretty little hands with business or matters of state. (Never mind that poor women have always toiled with their hands.)

It was in the eighteenth century, when a collection of colonies decided that they were being treated unjustly, that the

American woman's fight for equal treatment began. We've been left out from the beginning. In 1776 Abigail Adams wrote her husband, John, who was attending the Continental Congress in Philadelphia, "In the new code of laws, remember the ladies and do not put such unlimited power into the hands of the husbands." John Adams replied, "I cannot but laugh. Depend upon it, we know better than to repeal our masculine systems." And the men convening there drafted the Declaration of Independence, which states that "all *men* are created equal."

Yes, shortly after the "all men are created equal" line, it became self-evident that we women were somehow not. We weren't allowed to vote for the first president, or the second. In fact, it wasn't until the thirtieth president that we finally got to cast our vote, and we only got that right because in the late 1800s the women's suffrage movement began to demand it.

The Early Twentieth Century

In January 1917, when we still didn't have the right, a group of women sitting in the gallery during Woodrow Wilson's State of the Union address unfurled a large yellow banner asking, "Mr. President, what will you do for woman suffrage?" and women started demonstrating in front of the White House. By July of that year, an annoyed President Wilson was tired of all the demonstrating and started arresting the suffragists. Rather than giving up, they rallied. One of the movement's leaders, Alice Paul, went on a hunger strike in jail, and they tied her down and force-fed her three times a day for three weeks. When she was released from prison, she fought harder. Finally, President Wilson got the point and said he would support women's right to vote. The Nineteenth Amendment to the Constitution was ratified in 1920.

In 1921, Alice Paul drafted what she considered the logical next step, a simple amendment: "Men and women shall have equal rights throughout the United States and every place subject to its jurisdiction." In 1923, an empathetic male introduced it before Congress. Here we are almost a century later, and we *still* do not have equality of rights under the law.

World War II

The 1930s saw a chastened nation enter an age in which survival became a larger issue than social progress. Women in the workplace were frowned upon, as they would be taking a job that might go to a husband and father, but when they were *needed* during World War II, women were actively encouraged and lionized by the media for filling male roles. So many men were off to war that women were hired for the kinds of higher-paid, often heavy labor jobs that they'd never have been offered a decade earlier. Women could help win the war by working, and six million Rosie the Riveters went into the workforce in higher paying industrial jobs.

It didn't last. When the boys came marching home, the girls were expected to move out of the way: "Give me back my wrench, and get back into the house where you belong." Though 98 percent of women polled at the time said they would like to use the skills they had acquired and continue working, one out of every four lost her factory job. In another poll in 1945, 57 percent of women and 63 percent of men said that married women whose husbands earned enough shouldn't be *allowed* to work.

Hearth and Home Should Bring Happiness

In the 1950s, a campaign every bit as manipulative as the one that gave birth to Rosie the Riveter tried to sell women on the idea that ultimate happiness and satisfaction could be achieved only by devoting one's energies fully to home and hearth. Magazines such as *McCall's* and early television shows pushed an image of family togetherness in which the male ruled supreme and the woman, in her starched apron (to be removed in favor of something a little sexier before the husband's return in the evening) was intended to find her fulfillment by concentrating on the children and the nest, to the exclusion of all else.

The suburban tract house was filled with a gleaming array of modern appliances. These "advances" and workload somehow just weren't as fulfilling as the ads and articles promised, and physicians began prescribing more and more barbiturates and tranquilizers as women began having "nervous breakdowns" in droves. Psychiatrists and pundits proclaimed that women who wanted more were maladjusted and frigid, and probably to blame for everything from juvenile delinquency to homosexuality.

In 1959 Betty Friedan's *The Feminine Mystique* proposed that the problem with women's lives might be their circumstances rather than themselves. And then, with the advent of the birth control pill, a woman was no longer at the mercy of her fertility.

In 1964 Title VII of the Federal Civil Rights Act was passed making it unlawful to discriminate against any individual because of race, color, religion, sex, or national origin in matters of employment. Ironically, gender was added to Title VII by conniving lawmakers in hopes of spoiling its chances for passage. Fortunately, the effort failed and Title VII passed.

Throughout the 1960s and 1970s, women continued to enter the workforce, and those who enrolled in institutions of higher education increasingly strove for something besides what used to be scathingly referred to as the "MRS degree" [the quest for a husband]. They liberated themselves from their girdles and bras, and in the let-it-all-hang-out atmosphere of the times, more and more women began to simply talk to one another about their issues. As they shared life experiences and concerns, a collective epiphany happened: *It's not just me.* And the personal became political.

The ERA and Its Backlash

In 1972, the Equal Rights Amendment [ERA] actually passed Congress after forty-nine years of trying—and seemed set to have at least thirty-eight states ratify it into law. Then in 1973, with *Roe v. Wade*, the United States Supreme Court declared abortion to be a private matter between a woman and her doctor. Everything is heading in the right direction, right?

Nope—enter the backlash. The ERA, it was said, would legislate single-sex education out of existence, make government-funded abortions a necessity, subject women to the draft, and make single-sex public toilets illegal. Women such as Phyllis Schlafly added their voices to the chorus of fear and loathing, and suggested that a radical minority of women were demanding societal changes that "normal" women were not willing to support. Not only did the amendment fall three states short of passage, "women's libbers" and "feminists" were branded bad people.

For the next twenty-five years, "women's libbers" and "feminists" were demonized, and more and more women were subversively coerced into closing their mouths and settling for what our male leaders have deemed best for us since 1776. . . .

Women Are the Majority

I'm here to tell you we're the majority—our nation is now 51 percent girls and women, 49 percent boys and men, and given the strength of our numbers, I believe we *can* and *must* be honest about our needs and desires and *bold* in our quest for equality. We must not accept the idea that we are a "special interest group," that our pregnancies are "disabilities," and that our work efforts don't measure up dollar for dollar to men's. What's good for us is good for all. We can demand to be heard and we can demand that our wishes be acted upon.

So, here we sit in the breaking dawn of the twenty-first century, and we've actually taken a step (or two) backward.

Sure, we've come a long way from the 1876 ruling by a Minnesota court that decreed women did not need access to a legal education because they were too busy taking care of their children to study. But here it is 2007 and the Supreme Court is down to one woman, *Roe v. Wade* is in danger of being overturned, and we women are still being kept in our place by men in leadership positions deciding what's best for us, all the while maintaining the status quo.

So, what does "women's rights" mean to a woman in the twenty-first century? What women want today is certainly different from what it was 100 years ago, but it's also radically different from the wants of our mothers and our mothers' mothers. It's not about burning bras, or about bashing men. We're women with a different set of needs than those who came before. But what are those needs? What's missing from our lives? Where is the playing field not level? And what are our *actual* legal rights?

Career and Motherhood

In a September 2005 *New York Times* article headlined "Many Women at Elite Colleges Set Career Path to Motherhood," reporter Lisa Belkin stirred the pot by suggesting that many women at the nation's most elite colleges aspired to play the "traditional female role" after college, putting aside careers in order to make raising children their main commitment. One young woman (a Yale pre-law student with a 4.0 average) said her mother had always told her that she'd have to choose between career and motherhood because "you can't be great at both at the same time."

Belkin's survey of Yale undergraduates found that a whopping 60 percent said they'd cut back or stop working once they had children. The piece was followed by a tidal wave of letters that reflected divergent views from both men and women. . . .

In talking to women from across the nation—young, old, fat, thin, rich, poor, famous, and famous only to their husbands and kids—I've discovered that today gender inequality is still rampant, in both transparent and covert ways. What women want are improvements in areas of social equality, domestic obligations, and employment opportunities. . . .

Are Women Stepping Back?

Our laws are meant to assist us in the pursuit of happiness, but are they helping us do that? Have we become complacent, not because we're not concerned, but because we've become so busy keeping the balls in the air and food on the table that we don't have time to make it better? Have we settled into our routines and become a group of women who feel responsible to the demands of others—our husbands, our children, our parents, our bosses—and forgotten about ourselves?

Why have our voices gone quiet? Have we taken one step forward and two steps back by becoming the we-can-do-it-all gender, the ultimate "wonder women"—accepting our lot and spinning faster and faster, changing our hats with every spin? Why have we lost the fire of our foremothers? My fear is that younger women today are taking their rights for granted and do not understand that the laws that empower us, such as *Roe v. Wade*, which granted us control over our bodies, were not always here and are in danger of being taken away. Someone spoke up and fought for those rights, and many of them are quietly falling away like petals from a flower.

It's daunting how much easier it is to erase rights we have than gain new ones. If we don't protect what we have, our daughters will be left worse off than we are. How can we help our daughters protect and strengthen our rights, setting them on a path to reaching their full potential? How can we help our sons develop into men who are caring and aware? How can we help ourselves today?

These questions encourage us to find out who we are as women, what we want, and how we can do our part to follow that dream. They can only be answered by contemplating how far we have (and have not) come and by examining which rights we still need to fight for and who should be on the front lines of those battles. And the answers make the case for us to become the most fulfilled, empowered women we can be, transforming ourselves from a group that follows to a group that leads and *unites*. In this divided nation, I can think of no more important task.

Appendices

Appendix A

The Amendments to the U.S. Constitution

Amendment I: Freedom of Religion, Speech, Press, Petition, and
                  Assembly (ratified 1791)
Amendment II: Right to Bear Arms (ratified 1791)
Amendment III: Quartering of Soldiers (ratified 1791)
Amendment IV: Freedom from Unfair Search and Seizures
                  (ratified 1791)
Amendment V: Right to Due Process (ratified 1791)
Amendment VI: Rights of the Accused (ratified 1791)
Amendment VII: Right to Trial by Jury (ratified 1791)
Amendment VIII: Freedom from Cruel and Unusual Punishment
                  (ratified 1791)
Amendment IX: Construction of the Constitution (ratified 1791)
Amendment X: Powers of the States and People (ratified 1791)
Amendment XI: Judicial Limits (ratified 1795)
Amendment XII: Presidential Election Process (ratified 1804)
Amendment XIII: Abolishing Slavery (ratified 1865)
Amendment XIV: Equal Protection, Due Process, Citizenship for All
                  (ratified 1868)

The Amendments to the U.S. Constitution

Amendment XV: Race and the Right to Vote (ratified 1870)
Amendment XVI: Allowing Federal Income Tax (ratified 1913)
Amendment XVII: Establishing Election to the U.S. Senate
                   (ratified 1913)
Amendment XVIII: Prohibition (ratified 1919)
Amendment XIX: Granting Women the Right to Vote (ratified 1920)
Amendment XX: Establishing Term Commencement for Congress
                   and the President (ratified 1933)
Amendment XXI: Repeal of Prohibition (ratified 1933)
Amendment XXII: Establishing Term Limits for U.S. President
                   (ratified 1951)
Amendment XXIII: Allowing Washington, D.C., Representation in the
                   Electoral College (ratified 1961)
Amendment XXIV: Prohibition of the Poll Tax (ratified 1964)
Amendment XXV: Presidential Disability and Succession
                   (ratified 1967)
Amendment XXVI: Lowering the Voting Age (ratified 1971)
Amendment XXVII: Limiting Congressional Pay Increases
                   (ratified 1992)

Appendix B

Court Cases Relevant to the Nineteenth Amendment

United States v. Susan B. Anthony, 1872

Susan B. Anthony was arrested for voting in the 1872 presidential election. Anthony was hoping the courts would find that the newly passed Fourteenth Amendment would guarantee women the right to vote. Judge Ward Hunt of the Circuit Court of the United States for the Northern District of New York found her guilty, declaring that the Fourteenth Amendment did not protect her.

Bradwell v. Illinois, 1872

In this Supreme Court case, the Court upheld an Illinois law restricting state bar membership to men. This ruling prevented married woman Myra Colby Bradwell from practicing law.

Minor v. Happersett, 1874

In this Supreme Court case, Virginia Minor was accused of voting illegally in the 1872 presidential election. The Court decided that suffrage was not a privilege intended by the Constitution, therefore women did not have the right to vote.

Kaiser v. Stickney, 1880

This case is notable because it represents the first time a woman was allowed to argue a case in front of the Supreme Court. Belva Lockwood had been allowed to join the Supreme Court bar through special legislation passed by Congress. Fourteen months after joining the bar, she appeared with another attorney before the justices to argue this case.

The National Woman's Party Trials, 1917

In 1917, members of the National Woman's Party picketed for woman suffrage. Over the course of several months, many women, including well-known suffragist Alice Paul, were arrested and tried for obstructing the sidewalk.

Barkley v. Pool, 1919

In 1917, Nebraska's governor signed a legislative act giving women the right to vote in municipal and presidential elections. Opponents tried to overturn the law through a referendum petition drive that many claimed was illegal. The Nebraska law was suspended while *Barkley v. Pool* made its way to the Nebraska Supreme Court, which upheld the decision that the petition drive to overturn the legislative act was fraudulent.

Lesser v. Garnett, 1922

This case challenged the Nineteenth Amendment; it was brought by states that had refused to ratify. These states argued that this amendment added so many to the electorate that it took away their political independence. The Supreme Court stated that the Nineteenth Amendment did not change the electorate any more than had the Fifteenth Amendment, which gave black males the right to vote.

Adkins v. Children's Hospital, 1923

In a step back for women, Supreme Court Justice George Sutherland wrote in his opinion that the Nineteenth Amendment, in giving women the right to vote, also gave them the right to "liberty of contract" like men. This right to "liberty of contract" gave rights to the business owner instead of the worker. This decision struck down a minimum wage law for women in Washington, D.C.

Breedlove v. Suttles, 1937

This Supreme Court case dealt with voting poll taxes in Georgia. The Court upheld that poll taxes were constitutional and that the Nineteenth Amendment did not have any bearing on poll taxes.

For Further Research

Books

Bonnie S. Anderson, *Joyous Greetings: The First International Women's Movement, 1830–1860.* New York: Oxford University Press, 2000.

Jean H. Baker, *Sisters: The Lives of America's Suffragists.* New York: Hill and Wang, 2006.

Mari Jo Buhle and Paul Buhle, eds., *The Concise History of Woman Suffrage: Selections from "History of Woman Suffrage," by Elizabeth Cady Stanton, Susan B. Anthony, Matilda Joslyn Gage, and the National American Woman Suffrage Association.* Urbana: University of Illinois Press, 2005.

Sue Davis, *The Political Thought of Elizabeth Cady Stanton: Women's Rights and the American Political Traditions.* New York: New York University Press, 2008.

Ellen Carol DuBois, *Harriot Stanton Blatch and the Winning of Woman Suffrage.* New Haven, CT: Yale University Press, 1999.

———, *Woman Suffrage and Women's Rights.* New York: New York University Press, 1998.

Estelle B. Freedman, *No Turning Back: The History of Feminism and the Future of Women.* New York: Ballantine Books, 2002.

Constance Jones, *1001 Things Everyone Should Know About Women's History.* New York: Doubleday, 1998.

Fiona Macdonald, *Women in Peace and War, 1900–1945.* Chicago: Peter Bedrick Books, 2001.

Susan E. Marshall, *Splintered Sisterhood: Gender and Class in the Campaign Against Woman Suffrage.* Madison: University of Wisconsin Press, 1997.

Rebecca Mead, *How the Vote Was Won: Woman Suffrage in the Western United States, 1868–1914.* New York: New York University Press, 2006.

Kate O'Beirne, *Women Who Make the World Worse: And How Their Radical Feminist Assault Is Ruining Our Families, Military, Schools, and Sports.* New York: Sentinel, 2006.

Dorothy Schneider and Carl J. Schneider, *American Women in the Progressive Era, 1900–1920.* New York: Facts on File, 1993.

Lois Duke Whitaker, ed., *Voting the Gender Gap.* Urbana: University of Illinois Press, 2008.

Carol Lynn Yellin and Janann Sherman, *The Perfect 36: Tennessee Delivers Woman Suffrage.* Memphis, TN: Iris Press, 1998.

Periodicals

Brenda Betts, "Symbolism and Imagery in the Woman's Suffrage Movement," *Social Studies Review,* vol. 46, no. 1, October 2006.

Karen Breslau, "Now This Is Woman's Work," *Newsweek,* October 15, 2007.

Nancy Burkhalter, "Women's Magazines and the Suffrage Movement: Did They Help or Hinder the Cause?," *Journal of American Culture,* vol. 19, no. 2, Summer 1996.

Dorian Friedman, "Forgotten History in the Finger Lakes," *U.S. News & World Report,* April 5, 1998. www.usnews .com.

Jane E. Schultz, "New Women of the New South: The Leaders of the Woman Suffrage Movement in the Southern States," *Women's Review of Books,* April 1, 1994.

Nancy Shute, "Feminist Fatale," *U.S. News & World Report,* August 5, 2007.

Kenneth T. Walsh, "A Learning Experience," *U.S. News & World Report*, September 28, 2007.

Sarah Wilkerson-Freeman, "The Second Battle for Woman Suffrage: Alabama White Women, the Poll Tax, and V.O. Key's Master Narrative of Southern Politics," *Journal of Southern History*, May 2002.

Internet Sources

Robert Cooney, "Taking a New Look—The Enduring Significance of the American Woman Suffrage Movement," *Maryland Institute for Technology in the Humanities*. http://mith.umd.edu.

Emma Goldman, "Woman Suffrage," *Anarchism and Other Essays*, 1910. http://xroads.virginia.edu.

Him [pseud.], *How It Feels to Be the Husband of a Suffragette*, *American Memory from the Library of Congress*, 1915. http://memory.loc.gov.

Time, "As Maine Goes . . . ," September 5, 1960. www.time.com.

Vogue, "The School for Voters," September 15, 1917. www.oldmagazinearticles.com.

Web Sites

History.com, www.history.com. This History Channel site contains a detailed section on Women's History Month, information on women's suffrage, a timeline, a listing of women's achievements, and a women's facts and figures page.

Library of Congress, www.loc.gov. The Library of Congress Web site includes extensive materials on the subjects of women's suffrage and women's history. Many different history collections contain suffrage material, including photographs, print media, and Web casts.

National Women's Hall of Fame, www.greatwomen.org. This Web site contains hundreds of biographies of women who have contributed to American society in the fields of government, the arts, business, science, and education.

National Women's History Museum, www.nwhm.org. This history site contains an image library, a timeline, and a quiz, along with detailed information on the history of women's suffrage. The site also contains information on women's history, including women in industry, women in World War II, women in education, and other topics.

Spartacus Educational, Women's Suffrage, www.spartacus.schoolnet.co.uk/USAsuffrage.htm. This U.K. educational Web site contains an overview of the American women's suffrage movement. Extensive lists of names are detailed, along with internal links to other suffrage information. Information on the connection between British and American suffrage is also available.

Index